Finally, a book that talks to working mothers with warmth, wit and intelligence! Rachel's nail honest.

Her experience as a coach and real depth to this book. Wit humour and heaps of sense, tl who have both work and play·

Shaparak Khu̇ɪ̇ṣaṉu̇., ..

A working mother's survival guide! I wish I'd had this book when I was pregnant, and then experiencing the emotions, challenges and mental load that comes with juggling motherhood in all stages as well as a career. To know you are not alone in feeling all the feels is everything when you are in the thick of it!

Louisa Laudham, Chief People Officer,
Manolo Blahnik

I *flowed* through this book in three sittings, and genuinely felt like Rachel was sitting there with me coaching me while I read! I am so excited for all the women this is going to support on so many levels.

Jennifer Shepard, Senior Director, Getty Images

It is the *exact* book I needed when preparing for my first maternity leave and a must read for all your female colleagues, friends and family members that want to be great mums just as much as they want to continue rocking it in their careers.

Sophie Bishop, HR Director, UK and US, Euronext

For any mother adapting to their 'new normal' and for any employer who wants the best of their employees, I urge you to read this book!

Sarah Ray, Head of Podcast Sales,
Media Industry

There's a huge amount in here not just for mothers but for dads and partners too. Rachel Morris's empathy, compassion, and real insight gave me a different and hugely useful view on the issues so many brilliant working mums face.

Jonathan Samuels, Sky News presenter / broadcaster / journalist

Having children is like no other experience… It's difficult to prepare for, so having techniques and coping mechanisms in place for handling the transition is imperative! This book is full of practical ways to help yourself through the transition and gives the tools you need to take on your new identity. This book is perfect for giving reassurance and knowing that you're not alone.

Jessica Heagren, Careers After Babies Founder and Author

This is a must have for anyone bringing a baby into their family, whilst committed to continuing their career. The juggle is real, and Rachel helps unpack many of the universal challenges experienced by working mothers.

Elizabeth Cowper, Founder / CEWoMo, Ludo

I hope you enjoy!
Rachel

Working Mother

Simple coaching strategies for success at work and home

Rachel Morris

First published in Great Britain by Practical Inspiration Publishing, 2024

ISBN   9781788606141   (hbk)
        9781788606158   (pbk)
        9781788606172   (epub)
        9781788606165   (mobi)

Want to bulk-buy copies of this book for your team and colleagues? We can customize the content and co-brand *Working Mother* to suit your business's needs.

Please email info@practicalinspiration.com for more details.

Dedication

To my amazing children, Wilfred and Oswald. I hope this book helps people you love one day. You're both incredible, and I can't wait to see the positive impact you have on this world. Thank you so much for making me a working mother.

And to Dominic, my teammate. Words can't say how much you mean to me. Thank you for being by my side every single step of the way.

Contents

Table of figures

Acknowledgements

It may take a village to bring up a child, but it takes an army to publish a good book.

My army has consisted of so many brilliant people without whom I simply couldn't have done this.

I must begin with the three brightest lights in my world.

Wilfred and Oswald. I am so proud of who you are and know that you are always loved. Thank you for everything you teach me.

Dominic. Everything I am and that I do is connected to you. Thank you for your unwavering support and love. Thank you too for never forgetting the 'challenge' I asked you to promise you'd bring to our relationship all those decades ago.

Thank you to my brilliant business partner, Howard Rich, who has been by my work-side for over 20 years. You are incredible and your unconditional support in this project has been priceless.

I'd also like to thank my colleagues at Motion Learning who provide brilliant coaching support to people every single day. You're inspirational.

Talking of inspiration, thank you to Practical Inspiration Publishing and especially to Alison Jones for your wisdom and guidance. Also to Carl French from The Endless Bookcase for making me believe I really had a good book in me, and for helping me to take those important initial steps.

And a huge thanks to all the wonderful friends, colleagues and clients who read my manuscript at different stages in its development. Your bold feedback, kindness of heart and generosity of time has been mind-blowing. I will be forever grateful.

But the final word of thanks has to go to all of the incredible working mothers I have had the absolute privilege to work with and learn from. Thank you for the trust you have placed in me, and for the experiences you have bravely shared in our coaching conversations. I respect you all so very much.

This book is testament to you, and to *your* brilliance.

Introduction

Dear Reader

I'm so pleased you are here, reading this book, because I believe it has much to offer you.

I understand how challenging it can feel to be a working mother – how relentless it can seem – how the number of conflicting expectations appear to multiply by the day. I know how hard it can be in these times to connect and anchor ourselves with the essence of who we are.

I know because I am a working mother.

I'm also a business coach and I support people navigating their own professional challenges. One of my kids says my job is to help people to be happier. I kind of like that as a Key Performance Indicator.

In 2012, I was approached by a national broadcaster asking for my help with a new initiative they were rolling out. 'Maternity Coaching' – supporting working women in their transition out of the workplace, into motherhood and back as working mothers.

At that time, I was the 'already-pregnant-again working mother of a six-month-old baby boy'. I'm not sure having children just over a year apart in age was the plan. 'Like buses' my partner said. 'None for ages, then two at once.'

Being self-employed, I'd returned to work part time when my eldest son was just over six weeks old. Our household required two incomes, and no maternity benefits dictated the need for me to return as soon as possible.

However, alongside the financial need for me to work, there was an internal one too. I *wanted* to work, just as much as I wanted to be a mother.

Now there's a real dilemma. But one that I believe, with insight, clarity and determination, is completely doable.

I promise that by the time you finish this book we will have explored this conundrum together – how to be great at work and at home – and you will have found answers that work for you and your life.

To guide you in finding your answers, I will be drawing on experience gained from nearly two decades of practising as a coach.

I have heard many stories, walked with incredible people on their individual journeys, shared times of great successes, and supported times of deep stress and sadness.

Although this book is focused on you – the working mother – I do fully recognize that *all* working parents can find this transition daunting. No matter who they are or how they become a working parent. I support mothers, fathers, biological and non-biological parents in my coaching practice, and have worked hard to understand the transition *all* working parents experience.

At the back of this book you'll find the Parental Transition Model© (see Appendix A) which I developed with my colleagues at Motion Learning. It clearly shows three distinct phases in the transition working parents experience in the months where they welcome a child into their lives.

Each phase has different needs and requires a different coaching response. Take a look for yourself when you are ready to see the detail.

How to get the most from this book

I wrote this book with the intention of it being useful. I want you to feel like you can dip in and out of it, and I'd love nothing more than for it to be really well thumbed.

In this book, I refer primarily to the early days of working parenthood. But I believe it can be a manual for you as you progress to having children through all stages of their development – from entering school, through puberty and into adulthood.

I asked a friend of mine with adult children: 'What changes for parents as their offspring develop and grow?' He simply said: 'They will need you just as much Rachel, but it may be less frequently, but more intense when they do.'

How true that is, and it confirms that I – as a working mother – am still needed, still learning and still developing my skills. It sounds like I always will be.

So the principles you will learn in this book are timeless and, I believe, priceless.

To make it easy for you to come back to over time, every chapter has a different topic based directly on experiences women like you bring to coaching. They are grouped as sets of strategies to support you with different things. Written so you can choose the strategies that seem relevant to you at any given moment in time.

If you like to read books from cover to cover please do; if you prefer to dive into a chapter that really catches your attention then you can do that too. Whatever you feel works.

One friend read this book before it was published and said she didn't think the final chapter was 'the end'. Instead, it's a book to be revisited... and revisited.

Also, to help with this, every chapter has highlighted sections entitled 'Take a moment'. These contain practical activities to help you take the principle we've been looking at and apply it to your personal situation.

I want you not only to understand topics like 'control', but to know when and how to regain control on a practical level when you feel you need it. The 'Take a moment' sections are exactly designed for this.

These sections often suggest written reflection. So whether you write digitally or on paper, somewhere to capture your thoughts might be helpful. If you like writing on the pages of a book, then feel free to do that here. It's *your* book.

In the spirit of coaching, what you get out of this book will multiply exponentially if you are willing to put the effort in. Take the actions in the pages, reflect on the questions I pose, try out the ideas we come up with. We all know that if we want to change something, we start by doing something differently. You will be challenged to do this, and if you do, the positive impact will be plentiful.

You do not need to have prior experience of working with a coach to get the most from this book. I guide you through everything. But if you'd like to find out more about what coaching is, I've added some recommendations in the 'Further reading' section at the end of the book.

My dream

I have a recurring dream that one day I will see someone reading this book on a train. I will sit next to them and simply ask if it's any good. They will turn to me and say, 'It's amazing and it's completely changing the way I feel.' Maybe this person will be you. I hope so.

If you're ready to make choices and take control over your life as a working mother, sit back and get comfy, because now we are in this together. And we have work to do.

Rachel Morris, London UK, 2024

Part one
Your essential strategies

1
Endings

'Will I ever be the same again?'

I have a friend called Olivia who is fun, energetic and generous in thought and action. A working woman with a kind heart and a desire to do well.

The first time we met, her presence arrived in the room before she did. Confident, vivacious and engaging.

Heavily pregnant, and in so many ways truly rocking life.

Within a short while, I also realized I had also met a woman who was terrified about the prospect motherhood.

Why was she so scared? Because life was changing for her, in some ways forever.

As it quite probably is for you.

And that can be exciting *and* daunting.

What you know about life today might be different from how it has been, and how it will be. And because of this, the arrival of a child – a monumental change event – is undoubtedly inextricably linked with some loss.

That loss will come in all different shapes and sizes. For example, my partner and I recently went to a friend's birthday celebration, and we realized it was the first time we'd been to a party just by ourselves for about five years. It seems crazy even writing that, but that's the truth. Our reality. We had a brilliant time, and I realized just how much I still miss the opportunities to be just with him.

In the quiet, still moment as you read this, what comes into your mind? When you put your hand on your baby, how does your body feel?

You might feel calmness, quietness, space.

You might feel heaviness, concern, fear.

You might feel resistance, resentment, anger.

Or maybe you feel a combination of all these things at different moments in time.

That's OK. All are valid, natural and important, and I will show you why.

The vivacious, energetic friend I describe was nervous of losing the essence of who she was, in gaining something new and different. And that's quite a big thing to get your head around.

Learning to let go

I remember washing the baby clothes we'd bought before the arrival of our first son. Hanging them on the line and stepping back feeling like my heart was going to burst. I recall my partner standing next to me, and me saying how excited I was that I was finally going to have the chance to be called 'mum'. I suspect I didn't have a clue what that really meant, nor the responsibility and privilege that would come with it. But I did know that once it started that was a new name I could own, one way or another, forever.

Although I continue to feel my life is much richer since I became a parent, I'm also sometimes sad about the things I have let go of – or, in some instances, completely left behind. And it's not just nights out. Reflecting here today, one of the things I still feel sad about is the loss of aspects of my independence. My ability to be truly care-free without responsibilities to other people.

With gain often comes loss and it's important we address this directly together.

Have you thought about what you are letting go of in becoming a parent? Go back to those thoughts and feelings I encouraged a few moments ago. I wonder what they are telling you.

Maybe your baby is yet to arrive, and you are anticipating changes in the friendship dynamics around you. Or maybe your baby is here, and you recently went out with people you care about and realized how little you get the chance to see each other now.

Maybe you looked at your bank account and noticed how little spare there is in there, and that the holiday will need to wait for a little longer.

Maybe you're stopping work, and you are wondering what's going to replace it and how you feel about that.

Or maybe it's something else.

Whatever it is, it's perfectly understandable, but it may feel more or less comfortable for you.

In the text that follows is the first 'Take a moment' section I mentioned in the introduction. This is where we can get practical and think more deeply.

If now is the right time for you, please grab something to write on. If it isn't, then I suggest you will benefit from revisiting it later or in the future.

 Take a moment

I'd like you to develop a personal list of your 'losses'. Aspects of your existing life that you are concerned you could lose through parenthood. These may be permanent, or they might be temporary.

Think deeply, and try to *feel* your loss, not just logicize it. You'll limit your list if you do it this way. Ask yourself: What am I really worried or sad about losing and having to let go of?

To start you off, here is a list of frequent losses people share with me in coaching sessions:

- Freedom
- Fun
- Spare cash
- Space (physically and emotionally)
- Holidays
- Pastimes
- Time – with partners, family, friends
- Energy to do things
- Late mornings
- Sense of self

You may wish to write down some of these points or have different ones of your own you want to add to your list. Please feel free – it's yours, and the more robust it is the better.

Once you have written your list, I'd like you to write a number by each point from a scale of 0–10, where 0 indicates you are fine with the loss, 1 represents 'a little concerned about losing this' and 10 represents 'extremely concerned about losing this'.

Once completed please pause and reflect. What does your list tell you about how you are *really* feeling? See if you can use some descriptive words – for example, 'sad', 'excited', or 'nervous'.

When you've done this, simply pause and take a moment to think about what you have written.

It could be that you feel genuinely uncomfortable about some of the points this activity raises. In contrast, other things on your list you might already feel fine about letting go of.

I suspect when you look at your list there are also different levels of finality to the individual points – for example freedom may feel limited for a few years (along with sleep!) but when you think about it, you know that it's likely to return at some point in the future. Money comes and goes, and deep friendships typically weather the harshest of storms. Those friends who you see again after time has passed, after big events have taken place and it feels like no time at all since you were last together.

See, the thing about change is that it has a fluidity to it. Very little is static, and this really helps us when we think about the changes parenthood brings.

To aid our thinking and understanding of this, I want to introduce an important concept.

Think 'transition'

According to Bridges (2003), there is value in recognizing the very powerful distinction between change and **transition**.

Change is an event, but transition is our response to that event.

Let's think about this in relation to the arrival of a child.

Your child will have a day they physically arrive in your world.

However, we begin preparing ourselves for that specific event way before it happens. We begin to **transition** from the moment we find out we are expecting that child; we begin anticipating the impact of the change. We start working out what it is going to mean for so many different things – our homes, our work, our relationships, our lifestyles.

My own children have recently entered double digits, and I think I'm just about beginning to understand the impact their arrival has had on some aspects of my life. And why does it take time? Because this transitional response is gradual. We don't go from being a childless adult, to being suddenly fine about having a child in our lives.

It happens gradually – we *slowly* get used to it. A little like watching the tide go in and out. There's no sudden moment it changes, but it does – just subtly over a period of time slowly ebbing forwards and backwards.

One of the things we know about transition, about understanding and accepting the impact of change, is that we must start at the end – with what we are letting go.

The early phase of transition is all about letting go – and accepting that what has been is no longer how things are going to be. It's going to be different.

It's only by doing this that we can let go and ease into the change that is already afoot.

My friend Olivia really struggled with letting go of her freedom. I don't think she realized it until a long time after her children were born, but one day we were out, and it looked like it had hit her like a tonne of bricks.

She shared that she was so tired of always being responsible for someone or something. End-of-day collection, getting supper ready, washing... I recall her being really clear that it wasn't the individual tasks, but the overall sense of always having to be somewhere, doing something for someone else, which was overwhelming. She was so sad about her loss of energy, of glamour, of freedom.

Often, once we notice things like this, they can become even harder for a while. We bring them into our consciousness, and this can be uncomfortable.

However, I promise you that over time the intensity starts to change. As you begin to accept and allow these emotions, it can feel as though this intensity ebbs away. Often, even by simply acknowledging things, they can start to feel better.

Alongside the losses, you'll be relieved to know that you will also find there are things you *aren't* leaving behind at all – things you are taking with you, that may remain the same.

For example, I really believed my relationship would endure the arrival of a baby. Sure, the nights out would go for quite a while, but my 'teammate' would still be my 'teammate' – someone I could talk to, share my worries and stories with. He was one of my important constants.

When I work with clients like you in this particular transition, we begin by acknowledging how we feel about this time of transition. Just like you and I did a little earlier together. Identifying the joy and maybe the sadness, acknowledging the excitement but also the fears.

Then together, we move on to separate out what we are in fact losing, be it temporary or permanent, and what we are keeping with us. It's often a powerful process.

So, if you have the opportunity now to dig more deeply into what this change really means to you, here's something to try with the list you developed earlier.

 Take a moment

I suggest you now revisit your notes, and ask yourself these questions.

- What things am I *permanently* leaving behind? How do I really feel about this?
- What things am I *temporarily* leaving behind? When might I get them back?
- What things am I *in part* leaving behind? How do I really feel about this?
- What things (or parts of things) are *staying* and coming with me?
- And importantly, what things might I be *gaining* from this change?

How do you now feel looking at that list? Are any actions arising from your thoughts?

You may feel relief, or see a new perspective. There may be point you really want to explore further, or insight that can be used in dialogue with your people at home, or line manager at work.

Once you've reflected, ask yourself what you can do with this, and take a moment to draw out any actions you want to take.

Your list may be long, or it may be short.

What is for certain is that there will be losses, but there will be constants you have found too. And there will be some potential gains. Even in times of big change, we have these. It is the constants and the gains we can use to anchor ourselves against the headwinds when they come.

Remember my friend Olivia? When we boil down everything about her transition, it turns out there was something core to her feeling of instability.

Olivia was scared of losing her **identity.**

What makes you who you are?

Identity: Being, or feeling that you are, a particular type of person

Olivia still wanted to be 'Olivia' but she worried that becoming a mother would really change this.

Let's be truthful, becoming a parent *does* impact who we consider ourselves to be, and who others think us to be. I took years before I could settle into really accepting that I was the mother of two kids. It took ages to say, 'my children' even though my heart burst with pride from the moment I had them.

I suddenly had this new job title. And was unsure about what it really meant to me.

Experts have grappled for centuries with the question of what makes us who we are. I suspect every single human being has at some point asked themselves this question in their own way too. One thing we know is that we are constantly evolving – transitioning – being influenced by the people and events around us.

Swiss psychoanalyst Carl Jung beautifully articulated this by suggesting that becoming who you really is actually the privilege of a lifetime. Personally, I find this incredibly powerful and reassuring.

When I ask my own clients the question 'What makes you who you are?' they often come back with a list a something like this:

- Core values
- Beliefs (religious or other)
- Personality
- Gender
- Sexuality
- IQ/EQ baselines
- Background
- Upbringing
- Culture
- Friends
- Family
- Community
- Experiences
- Work
- Skills
- Knowledge
- Education
- Goals
- Ambitions
- Motivations
- Hopes
- Strengths
- Vulnerabilities
- Responsibilities
- Expectations

Moreover, there are still contributing factors such as the roles we choose to play. Or are expected to play. It's inevitable that at some point we will ask ourselves 'How do I behave now I am a mother? Is *this* what mothers are *supposed* to do?'

I wonder how *you* feel your identity will be affected by parenthood. What will change, and what will remain?

Some people find that in reality less changes than they anticipated. Because much of what makes you who you really are stays. Sure, it may change slightly – but the future doesn't erase the past.

You will most likely find that your identity grows and expands in the most exciting ways.

Olivia remains vivacious, energetic and generous in both work-mode and mother-mode. And my first night out in years with my partner proved to be the green shoot of something new. We had such a lovely time, we decided to make it happen again. And we have. Slowly and surely something I thought was lost has been found, and now it's back I love it more than ever.

If we want to transition effectively through times of change, then we must begin by facing and understanding what is ending and what isn't. We must acknowledge that we need to let go of some things, take other bits with us and pick up new bits along the way.

Knowing this will help you as you experience your own transition into working parenthood. And for much of the time I hope it provides useful insight and reassurance.

But we must be realistic, as there are times when you will still feel anxious, and possibly scared. Because stepping into the unknown can often be scary. So it's important we move on to think about how we support ourselves when we feel this way.

It's important we talk about **fear**.

2
Fear

'What if I can't do this?'

One day I was in a coaching room with a lovely dark-haired woman sitting in front of me. I vividly recall her wearing a beautiful bright yellow top, lighting up the room as she sat there in her chair.

Asking her how she was today, I saw her body tense, her eyes drop, and the yellow of her outfit begin to dull.

'What if I'm not a good mother?' tumbled out of her mouth as she looked at her lap, almost ashamed to utter these words

I paused.

'What if my child doesn't love me, and what if I can't take care of it?'

Pause.

Followed by 'I'm worried that I just can't do *any* of this? What if I *fail?*'

Quiet, dull tears.

Now this is a scary place to be. I've been there myself, and maybe you have too.

It's scary, but not uncommon. The transition into motherhood is fraught with lots of 'what ifs' and significant ones too.

And at that very moment in time, my client was *really* scared.

She was scared of what might happen to her. What she was embarking on. Too late to turn back.

You could see the fear in her face; you could feel it throughout her body.

Reading this, maybe you empathize and even share some of her fears?

Fear is an emotion that can rumble in the background. So together we are going talk about it – to bring our fears into the open and shed light on them. We are going to listen to what they are trying to tell us and see what we find.

Take a deep breath, and don't worry, I've got you.

Fear

Fear: An intense emotion stimulated by the detection of imminent threat

Have you ever been driving and had to suddenly slam on the break quickly, causing a rush of energy to wave through your body?

That was fear and your response to it.

Have you ever been walking alone down a dark street and started moving faster to get yourself home quickly?

That too, was fear and your response to it.

Have you ever felt uncomfortable by someone shouting on public transport, and decided to read your book with even more intensity in the hope that the shouting won't come closer to you?

Yes, surprise! That was fear and your response to it.

In each instance, the response is triggered by an actual, or perceived, threat: the threat of crashing, the threat of being vulnerable, the threat of getting involved in conflict.

But what's so threatening about motherhood? Do these big words really apply to something like the arrival of a child?

Yes, they do, and my client in her yellow top was experiencing this in all its glory.

Her baby – although yet to arrive – was posing a threat.

Threats are things that we believe will – or could – negatively impact us. Directly or, in the case of a baby, by its very presence.

Are you feeling 'threatened' by things at the moment? It's possible you are. You may experience this deeply and consistently. It may be light and fleeting.

I pulled together a list of the threats recent maternity clients have brought to coaching, so you can see what they tell me they experience.

- The threat of not getting enough sleep
- The threat of not earning enough money
- The threat of not being able to take good care of their baby
- The threat of existing relationships changing or being damaged
- The threat of a loss of 'self'
- The threat of no longer being good at work
- The threat of not being seen as a good mother
- The threat of not having time to do important or enjoyable things anymore
- The threat of losing lifestyle choices

Writing these down, I'm conscious of how strong and significant the list is. To me it shows how deeply our fears can be during the transition into parenthood.

My wonderful, but worried, dark-haired client was scared of almost all of these. No wonder her brightness was dimming.

Calling out our fears is a really useful way of starting to overcome them. If we bring them into the light, we can do something about them more easily than when they lurk in the dark depths of our hearts.

Take a look at the next 'Take a moment' exercise, which offers something for you to do to help identify any fears you may currently have. It may make you feel a little uncomfortable as it did my client. Try accepting and working with it if you can.

 Take a moment

Begin by writing down your responses to this statement:

'At this phase in my life, I am worried the following things could negatively affect me...'

For example, your maternity cover might be better than you, or your friend's opinion of you might change.

Then, for each point, ask yourself what the underlying 'threat' is. See if you can drill down and identify it.

For example, if your maternity cover is better than you, your employer may want to keep them on instead of you. This could feel like a threat to your livelihood, your reputation and/or your self-esteem.

Take time, work through your list with thought and consideration. This is an activity to help you identify the threats your brain believes it is facing. If you find it challenging, that's OK. The more we practise this, the easier it becomes as we increase our awareness levels each time.

Once you've done this, simply take a moment to digest and reflect upon how you now feel. Just notice what your brain and your body are saying to you.

You may feel more heightened, more worried – or not.

You may see answers or actions becoming clear – or not.

All responses are valid; for now we are just noticing which in itself is powerful.

Threats, whether acknowledged or not, *will* be causing you concern. Whether they 'should or shouldn't' is irrelevant, as fear overrides our logic making it temporarily ineffective.

This is why, when another person asks you not to be worried about something, it can have little meaning.

Threats also automatically set in motion a series of psychological (and physical) changes in us, and I think it's important we understand this.

It's a bit like a smoke alarm going off inside us.

The smoke alarm

I have a very irritating smoke alarm in my home. It's super sensitive. It goes off at the drop of a hat. I'm still very pleased this smoke alarm is there though, as it helps me to feel like we are safe. But I do wish it could tell the difference between a piece of bread being toasted and real danger.

You have a smoke alarm inside of you too. As do I.

Our smoke alarms kick off when they get the whiff of a 'threat'. Our brain receives a signal that basically says, 'my human might be in trouble' and it responds saying 'OK, don't worry, I'm on it'.

This part of our brain is called the amygdala, and it is there to keep us safe. My children call it their 'Guard Dog'.

The amygdala's job is to watch out for threats and to alert us when one is detected. It's your own personal smoke alarm.

At times our alarm works perfectly, but sometimes it's a bit over-sensitive – like the one in my hall. Either way, it won't stop sounding until we tend to it.

For example, if my alarm thinks the shouting in the tube carriage is a threat to me, my alarm won't calm down until either the shouting has stopped or until I have moved out of what I perceive as harm's way.

Common threats that working mothers tell me set the smoke alarm off, include concerns such as these.

- The safe arrival of their baby
- The effectiveness of their maternity cover at work
- Money
- Sorting effective childcare
- When and how to return to work
- Changes to relationships

Do you relate to any of these? I know I did when I was pregnant.

The secret is to tend to these things. That's how we calm the alarm down. Not to ignore them. If we do, they will only get louder.

But how?

Let me answer this by telling you about my friend Femi.

Femi was remarkably relaxed about the arrival of her first daughter. She'd developed a fluid birth plan, prepared as best she felt she could and was (literally) breathing her way into the days before her baby arrived. 'Then things took a turn. The baby arrived suddenly and in unexpected circumstances. At that moment in time, there was a real threat, and her smoke alarm sounded loudly and clearly.

She listened to it, got the help she needed quickly, and the baby was delivered safely.

In contrast, another friend was terrified about the birth of her child in the run up to her maternity leave. In the six weeks before her due date she developed birthing plans, scheduled Reiki appointments and bought packets of raspberry leaf tea. Her baby arrived on time, in hospital with limited pain control and her partner by her side.

This woman also listened to her fears and tended to them in the best way she could.

Listening to your alarm and responding is the key. Trying to avoid or ignore it only makes it louder.

Listening to your fears

Are you good at listening to yourself and your own needs? I know it can be hard at times.

I remember being out with some other new mums when my son was about seven months old.

At some point, I noticed I became uncomfortable. In myself and in my body. I felt a real need to hold my child close to me and recall my instinctive desire to pick him up and to put him into his sling.

(My alarm beginning.)

As the conversation continued, I felt increasingly uncomfortable, like I really needed to get away.

(My adrenal response suggesting I do something.)

I stayed a while longer and felt myself getting more and more uncomfortable – a little angry even.

(My alarm getting louder, concerned as it wasn't being heard.)

I made my excuses and left. I got us back home, held my baby close and wondered what had just happened. My alarm stopped sounding, and equilibrium was restored.

But what had threatened me? What was I fearful of?

Reflection of this specific situation has taught me that I was threatened by well-meaning comments from my friends, about things they were experiencing, things they were doing that I wasn't. This made me feel vulnerable and uncomfortable. It was all happening inside of *me*.

Ultimately, I feared failing. I feared not being a 'good enough' mum to my child. For some reason, I felt that by getting him home, warm, and holding him close, I would be doing a better job.

When I listened to this feeling, I acted, and things changed in me. I regained my equilibrium and my mind settled.

My alarm calmed.

So, let's listen to any fears *you* might be holding at the moment. See what they are trying to tell you and use this to determine your response. It's way better than being held hostage by it.

 Take a moment

Go back to your list from the previous exercise.

When you look at it, what do you think your fears are trying to *tell* you?

They might be telling you that you need to talk to someone, or that you need to find out the answer to a question.

They could be telling you that you need to make a plan about something. Maybe even a Plan B and a Plan C too.

Or... they might be telling you that you need to take care of yourself. Practise a bit of self-kindness, and take some time out just to stop.

Whatever comes to mind, just note your thoughts down.

I hope you'll now have a list of actions that you could take to help yourself to feel better. Be realistic: if your action feels too big, break it down again and again until you feel like you can take that first important step.

I hope you can see that when you tend to your alarm, there's often something you can do. It's natural to feel scared about so many parts of the transition you are experiencing, but the fear is telling you something useful – so listen.

We all feel scared at times. Every single new parent feels fear and I am told by much more experienced parents than me that this feeling never quite goes away, no matter how old and independent your children are. So lucky us. This lovely pit of the tummy feeling could well be here to stay.

And it is that feeling which can, in fact, make parenthood so wonderfully elemental.

Acknowledging fear, understanding what it is saying, noticing how we are experiencing it and tending to our needs all provide possible answers and actions.

Before closing this chapter, I want to bring into our conversation one more topic that working mothers frequently talk about.

And this one *often* induces fear and sends logical reasoning running out of the door.

'Mum guilt'

The heavy 'should have done, ought to have done, shouldn't have done, ought not to have done' relentless conundrum often articulated by mothers

Aah… good old mum guilt. That faithful friend that seems forever close by, and is always willing to get involved and lend us a hand.

There are so many places in this book where I could have chosen to put a spotlight on this, because it influences many of the topics we will talk about. Self-care, boundaries, our return to work, efficiency – to name just a few.

I'm choosing to put it here, because guilt is such a powerful trigger of the smoke alarm.

When did you last feel guilty? Personally, it was last night, when I left my children to watch TV after school, as I needed to take a work call.

I was 'supposed' to be reading with them instead and furthering their chances of a successful future.

My guilt manifested as a judgemental voice inside my head saying 'You should have said "no" to your call; you could have been better organized: they're going to fail in life and it will all be your fault for not reading enough with them… !'

Great.

As an emotion, guilt is considered to be one of the most complex. It's often articulated as an undesirable one that can leave people feeling heavy and uncomfortable.

In fact – as with most emotions – it has a really significant role. For example, guilt can often be the emotion that helps us to say sorry if we have hurt someone.

Feeling appropriately guilty for something we have done is important. But sometimes we feel guilty about things we haven't done, or we can feel disproportionately guilty about something that was only very small. Sometimes we can feel guilty about things we believe we 'should' have done.

And working motherhood is rife with things we feel we *should* have done.

There have been times when…

- I *should* have left the meeting when it overran to avoid being the last person to collect from nursery.

- I *should* have stayed at home with my child who was grumbling about a sore throat and not taken him into school so I could get into work.

- I *should* have cooked a wholesome meal for them as opposed to giving them a quick and easy sandwich.

- I *should never* have looked at my work emails – *ever* – while they were eating their breakfast.

One question:

Who says I *should*?

Who says I *should* have felt guilty yesterday? My children didn't seem bothered. In fact they were delighted to watch TV instead of reading. The person on the other end of my call was grateful I could find time for them. It really made a positive difference.

So who says I *should* be feeling guilty – other than *me*?

This changes something.

Why? Because this acknowledgement has the potential to empower me. It has the potential to make me pause – for just long enough – to make a choice about whether I need to feel guilty about something or not.

And if I do – great. I apologize, I change my action, I learn.

And if I don't – even better. I choose to say thank you very much, but no. I will not feel guilty. I choose to carry on.

So please, don't assume that guilty feeling in the pit of your body automatically means you've done something wrong, or not done something you should have done. Next time, you feel it ask yourself one simple question.

Who says?

The answer will tell you whether indeed you've something to feel guilty about.

Or not.

By the way, if you cast your mind back to the start of this chapter, I told you about a client of mine who was riddled with the fear of failing. And alongside this fear, she was full of voices readying her to feel guilty about not being a 'good enough' mum.

Well, I can tell you she *is* a good mother, she loves her child who loves her back dearly, and she is not failing. Also, what's great is that she knows this too.

Her yellow top is bright and smiling once again.

3
Learning

'Will I ever know what I'm doing?!'

I was sitting with my partner in a living room in North London. Around us in a circular pattern were 14 other wide and open faces. Seven of them had big bumps resplendently poking out from underneath their clothes.

All of us were focused on a more experienced mother with some little knitted toy boobs on the floor in front of her.

This evening we were talking about breast-feeding.

Just an hour earlier, I'd been helping a global executive team thrash out their new five-year strategy.

'Before we start… I'd like to ask you each a question,' she said beaming.

'What's your parenting style going to be?'

Tumbleweed.

'Our what?!!' I exclaimed loudly once back to the safety of our home. 'I don't know what one is let alone realize I'm supposed to have one!'

My partner looked at me blankly.

Let me ask *you* a simpler question. What do you not yet know that you are going to need to know?

Exactly. Tricky isn't it?

I *know* that your goal is to be a good mother, and a good working mother. But how can we possibly settle into becoming this when we are unsure of what it really entails?

One of my children told me I was a good mum recently, which made me feel very nice. I smiled and said thanks. Inside I was thinking 'That's lucky isn't it, because I'm not sure I have a clue what I'm doing half the time… '

And that's why this is our next thing to tackle. How we **learn**.

Learning

To learn: To develop knowledge or skill in something new

When a child first learns to walk, they begin by 'just having a go'. Presumably assuming they can do it.

Then they fall flat on their bottoms realizing they can't. Sometimes at this point they cry.

Over time they try again and again, maybe reaching out to hold anything that might help them – maybe a sofa edge, a welcome hand or any random bag or bottom that might be in the vicinity.

Then eventually they get good enough to do it all by themselves, and it becomes so automatic they forget it was ever hard.

This is learning, which many researchers agree broadly follows a pattern based on a combination of awareness and capability (see Gordon and Burch, 1974).

The process often starts before the learning even clearly begins. This is the point at which we don't know what we don't know. We are completely unaware and often **blissfully ignorant**.

So many aspects of parenting are like this – until we are experiencing something directly, we can read about it, chat to friends about it to get a sense. But we can't truly know for certain until we have the experience first-hand.

Almost every single client I have worked with through their maternity transition has said 'Why didn't anyone tell me it was *really* going to be like this?' My answer? Because no one could.

That's the joy – and the limitation – of being 'blissfully ignorant'.

But over time things can change, and when they do we become aware of what we don't know. The question about my 'parenting style' is an example of this shift. I was suddenly very aware of what I didn't know. My blissful ignorance had turned into **acute awareness**.

Now *that's* not a nice feeling. However, it's an essential part of growth. We can only change something once we are aware of it.

When clients experience this change, they frequently describe it as a place that can feel exposing and sometimes uncomfortable.

I remember one of my clients returning to work six months after the arrival of her baby. About two weeks in we had a session, and she looked absolutely exhausted.

Through tears she quietly said 'I feel like I'm just failing at absolutely everything. I'm a bad mother, a rubbish leader, a terrible partner, and an absent friend.' She felt so vulnerable about many aspects of her life, and like she couldn't do anything that was expected of her.

Maybe you feel like this at times? I know her story isn't uncommon.

This is an example of her being acutely aware about some really important things. And although this can be an uncomfortable or even painful place to find ourselves in, it's essential when it comes to moving forward, learning and growing.

Fortunately, we don't necessarily have to feel this way for long because learning isn't a static thing. I went from not even knowing I needed to have a parenting style, to freaking out about what mine was going to be, and on to developing one of my own – with practice and experience.

I became **increasingly confident**.

As we learn and practise new things we typically increase our ability levels. We 'get better' at whatever it was we weren't good at.

When clients hit this place, they articulate an 'easing of pressure'. It's like the stress valve has been released, and although still very aware of what they are doing, they report it feeling like they are making progress.

I remember when both my children were under 16 months… my friend asked me if I wanted to go to a 'sing along' together.

I started getting us ready literally two hours before we needed to leave as I couldn't begin to work out how I was going to have all three of us clean, dressed, fed and ready to leave the house by 9am.

Within weeks I'd managed to slowly cut that time in half. I still wasn't nailing it but was getting better for sure. I was becoming more confident. I was doing what I needed to, but still with care and applied thought.

Then I don't know what changed, but I got to a point where I simply didn't need to think about how to leave the house. The hours of early planning seemed to just diminish without me noticing. I just started to get us all ready, pick up my bags and go.

At this point I was **quietly effective**.

From an observer's perspective the shift into this quiet, effective place is often quite seamless and can go by unnoticed.

It's a lovely place for the learner to be, especially after the effort they've usually put in to get there. It's important to have moments to acknowledge the wins in this space.

This is the pattern of life – learning, and moving, changing, experiencing, and growing.

And this is the underpinning pattern of *how* we learn.

Can you relate to this? I wonder what things spring to mind for you when you reflect on this.

The 'Take a moment' activity may help you to capture your thoughts on this.

 Take a moment

Without judgement (I know that can be hard), take a few minutes to begin noting down all the things you feel you aren't doing well at the moment.

When you've finished your list, take a moment to think about how you feel looking at it.

You might feel sad, you may feel relieved, or any number of other emotions may spring to your mind instead. They are all valid.

That's all you need to do for now. Let your thoughts settle, and we will come to this again shortly.

Learning is a process. We move from not knowing to knowing. From not being able, to being able. And sometimes we make this shift and sometimes we get stuck.

If we want to increase our chances of progress though, I recommend we all get ourselves a **helping hand**.

Your helping hand

There are times I *really* need a helping hand. I needed one over the weekend when I couldn't work out how to stop my children winding each other up. I needed one this morning when I felt completely overwhelmed by how to navigate an important family dilemma.

We all need a helping hand at times to enable us to get *better* at understanding, navigating or doing something.

But how do we get 'better' at something? I got 'better' at getting out of the house with two very young children by doing it again and again, with a friend at my side.

In general, we get better by:

- knowing what 'better' looks like – i.e. having a goal to work towards;
- having the information or resources necessary to achieve that goal;
- having the helping hand of support from people as we climb;
- having the opportunity to 'have a go', to try things out, and to keep practising; and
- having a moment to reflect and capture our progress.

And based on this, the kinds of things we need are:

- a clear goal;
- resources and information;
- experience, practice and reflection; and
- support and guidance.

These are the gifts a helping hand will offer us. And we all need them when we are learning.

 Take a moment

Go back to the list you wrote a little earlier (your list of the things you don't think you're doing well.). For now, simply pick **one thing** from that list which you consider a priority to improve. Maybe because it's the most difficult, or because it's the one that matters most, or maybe because it's a 'quick win'.

Then with that one thing in mind, follow this process.

1. What would 'better' look like for you? Note: I'm not asking you what 'perfect' looks like, just better. (For example, shaving 30 minutes off my getting-out-of-the-house time would have been 'better'.)
2. What do you not have access to that you know would help you? What knowledge, information or resources do you believe would make this better. (For example, understanding how other people managed to get themselves out of the house helped me with new ideas. Having certain things packed the night before, or already in the car helped me in the morning when things were busy. Having a flexible starting time worked too – between 8:30 and 8:45am. It helped me feel like I was still doing OK.)
3. Who do you need to help or support you? What requests do you have and of whom? (For example, I needed help from my partner both the night before and the morning of. Help with getting a bag ready, then popping it in the car on his way out the next morning. One less thing to think about or to carry...)

See if you can use these steps to begin to develop a new plan of action.

Change nothing and nothing gets easier. Change something, and a shift will happen one way or another. If it's not in the right direction, you can always shift things again.

Finally, once you've got your plan decide when and how you are going to test it out – plan it, and plan for your 'review' too. I once read it takes about six weeks for a new plan to be embedded enough for us to review. So stick with it, and after a good block of time *then* see if it is working for you or not.

When you are reviewing, ask yourself: what worked, and what didn't? What am I going to tweak for next time? Sometimes plans benefit from a 'tweak' more than an 'overhaul'.

Then repeat with another thing on your list. Again and again, over time choosing your priorities and shifting focus.

As a learning professional, I know that learning is a process. It's not always linear, and it's not always successful first time. But as with many things in life, we can give ourselves a little helping hand. Finding practical nudges to make our learning lasting.

Like a child learning to walk, the transition into parenting is one long learning journey. Every twist and turn new. Full of both vulnerability and eventual 'wins'.

But we *have* to walk through the space of vulnerability to get to the other side. It's something to be embraced and not feared because it is fundamentally essential.

And remember, we don't have to learn alone. One of my closest friends and I used to spend every Friday together when our kids were babies. We would share experiences, ask questions and overcome challenges together. Our babies would rattle around in the background, and we'd walk, talk, eat cake, talk, drink coffee, eat cake – and after 4pm we'd usually treat ourselves to a beer.

They were some of the most special days of my life. We were both learners and teachers to each other.

Learning can be challenging. But it doesn't have to be isolating.

4
Control

'I don't know what to do next!'

At 7:47am one morning, I was standing with my back against my bedroom door, holding it closed. My fingers were in my ears, my head was spinning, and my eyes were brimming.

Downstairs, my eldest was throwing his brother's shoes out of the front door onto the street, while the youngest was bowling his schoolbag across the hallway, sending books flying everywhere in the crossfire.

Recorder and violin practice were due to begin at school in exactly three minutes time. School is a seven-minute sprint from home.

I think it's fair to say that I wasn't feeling in complete control. I'm fine again now, but at 7:47am, I was certainly *not* fine.

On the contrary, I was incredibly **overwhelmed**.

Overwhelm

Overwhelm: To drown beneath a huge mass of something

When did you last feel overwhelmed? This morning my engulfing mass was a mix of shoes, violins, bags, recorders, books and yelling.

As a coach, one of the words I'm sensitive to is 'overwhelm'. When a client comes into a session and shows or articulates a sense of being overwhelmed it's critical to pick up on it.

Signs of overwhelm in people vary greatly – from anxious behaviour right through to a person 'stopping' and either freezing or collapsing. Personally I've grown to understand that my own signals of overwhelm start with things like trying to do too much all in one go, which results in me either not finishing anything or making mistakes.

I also know that I can 'freeze' when I'm overwhelmed. Remember, we talked about this in chapter 3. This morning, with my fingers in my ears, was an example of exactly this.

I wonder what your signals are that tell you you're experiencing overwhelm. Do you know?

If you struggle to identify them yourself, ask people close to you. They can often see it before we can. I suspect they can offer insight into what happens when *you* begin to get 'full up'.

I asked my partner, and he resisted the temptation to say, 'You just become a complete and utter nightmare.' Instead, he offered up 'You get a bit frantic, a little intense, slightly irrational.' Hmmm.

In your transition into working motherhood, there will be many times where you feel overwhelmed. It's a big time, so of course we can expect this to happen.

The danger, at times of overwhelm, is that the amygdala senses fear and we go into survival mode in response. If you have already read chapter 2 on 'Fear', you'll recall that this part of our brain has a core responsibility for spotting danger by way of trying to keep us safe. When it spots potential 'danger' it prepares us to respond to it.

People quite often arrive in coaching sessions in this state. With a look of 'I just don't know what to do next' about them, and appearing somewhat stuck.

This is normal. But it can also be uncomfortable and often counterproductive. Which is not what any of us want.

So, when a client shows that they are feeling overwhelmed, we have to do something to help them move past it.

What follows next is exactly how we tackle that. And I know this technique will be a lifesaver when *you* are next feeling overwhelmed.

Feeling full up

We all have things that 'fill us up'. You could be full up of feelings – for example, concern or responsibility. Or you could be full up of tasks you have on your mind – for example, rescheduling an appointment, placing an order, or making a decision about something.

This morning, the kinds of things that were filling me up ranged from 'I'm always late', via 'I'm neglecting my work' through to 'Why am I being shouted at?' and 'Will someone please just listen to me'.

All these things were 'filling me up'.

What's filling you up at the moment, I wonder?

Big things, small things, simple and complex things most probably. Because we *all* have stuff going on. Our modern world is complex, working life is complex and being a parent is most definitely complex. There's plenty of stuff out there that can't wait to 'fill you up'.

And this can lead to us feeling overwhelmed and lacking **control**.

Which is not ideal.

So how do we regain control when we feel overwhelmed? We follow these three significant steps.

1. We get what is in 'out', so we can see what we are dealing with.
2. We look at it all, work out what we want to take back and what we don't.
3. We prioritize what exactly we are going to do with the things we are taking back.

Step one: Let it out!

We begin by getting everything that is on our minds, and in our hearts, out. So we can see it and understand what we are dealing with.

 Take a moment

Take just two minutes to pour out your thoughts about what is 'filling *you* up' at this particular moment. Don't evaluate your thoughts or judge yourself – just write everything down.

This could be anything from 'I have to post a letter' or 'I've got to call the midwife' through to 'I need to write my handover' or 'I must move house before the baby arrives'.

It might be big or small, it might be easy to find a solution to, or difficult. Whatever the point – it is valid. Simply write it down.

Once you've done this, take a moment to reflect.

Notice how you feel after doing this. You may find that you feel relieved, or you may feel a little tense and anxious. Or maybe something different.

Don't judge your response, just notice it. We will be using this list again in a moment.

This action in itself can be incredibly powerful.

From a coaching perspective here, we are using a simple technique to help you step away a little from something you feel very attached to.

We're starting to put a little distance between yourself and the concerns you are holding. Providing you with the opportunity for a little distance, and maybe a slight change in your perspective. You might be experiencing this?

I often suggest to clients that they simply take a blank piece of paper and write their thoughts down when they're feeling overwhelmed. We can experience an instant shift from this simple action.

So remember this when you next need a quick fix.

Step two: Group it

The things that contribute to a feeling of overwhelm can seem messy, big and unruly.

They can feel like they are all clumped together – getting bigger and wilder.

So, in response, we want to clear things out, replacing the feeling of chaos and confusion with clarity and control.

We do this by separating out:

- things that belong only to us, that involve no one else;
- things we can share with another person and ask for support with; and
- things that can wait, that we can simply set to one side, for today; things that in the moment we can't – or do not need – to do something about.

In doing this we are using some key control principles. We're looking at what is in our 'direct', 'indirect' and 'no' control (Covey, 1989). Here's what the three terms mean in a little more detail.

Direct control: these are the things you do, in fact, need to control, face up to and do something with. Concerns that involve *just you*.

For example, stepping away from your desk to walk around and have some lunch, rescheduling the upcoming midwife appointment or having that conversation with your mum to tell her that you'd like to be alone with your partner at the birth.

This morning, I had direct control over my response to the situation. I chose to hide in the bedroom for two minutes. I chose this over shouting at the situation and adding to the noise.

Indirect control: these are the things you might want to share and ask for support with. These are things that need – or already involve – at least one other person.

For example, arranging meetings as part of the onboarding for your replacement, deciding the birth plan you want to write with your partner, or tying up the loose ends of a piece of work that requires input from another colleague before you can complete it.

This morning, I had indirect control over whether my kids apologized to each other and also over whether their music teacher would be irritated that they were late. We could apologize in the hope that it would help, but that was all.

No control: these are the things you need to set aside. For now. Either because you can, or because you have to. Often, we worry about things that right here, right now, we can do absolutely nothing about.

For example, how your baby will *actually* make its arrival, whether your child will live a long and happy life, or whether your replacement at work will be better or more liked than you.

Concerns that sit within our 'no control' often relate to past events – i.e. things that have happened (I wish I hadn't had an outburst in that conversation), are situational realities (I didn't plan on the baby deciding to arrive the day after I finished work), or future worries (What if I don't feel like I can both work and be a good parent? What will I do then?).

I realize these are examples of significant concerns. Just because something is not in our control at one point in time doesn't mean it isn't significant. It just means there's nothing we can do to influence or deal with that situation right now. Time may change things, but right here, right now there's nothing to be done.

This morning I had no control whatsoever over being late. There was no way I could magic a seven-minute sprint into a three-minute one. I'm not a good runner.

I ask clients to think about how it *feels* when they accept that they have no control over something. Often, they describe a sense of calm, a moment where the internal conflict stops. It's a bit like when you're stuck in traffic and realize that whether you like it or not there's nothing you can do. So you calm down and turn your attention to something else instead. This is what is feels like to accept that one of your concerns is something you genuinely don't control.

So these are the three possible responses to the points you have written on your piece of paper.

You will see how significant this is as you progress this 'Take a moment' activity.

Take a moment

Grab your pen again and look at your list from the previous 'Take a moment'.

It's time to separate your concerns into the three buckets.

- Put a 'D' by the points you have 'direct control' over. These are the things you will keep hold of, because you can, and need to, do something about them.
- Put an 'I' by the points you have 'indirect control' over. These are the concerns you do not need to – or can't – do by yourself. You need support with them.
- Finally, put an 'N' by the points you have 'no control' over. These are the concerns you need to – or can – set aside for today. They are a situational reality, or a future worry you can at the moment do nothing about.

Some of your concerns may split into smaller parts as you do this, which is absolutely fine.

For example, if you are worried about the birth of your baby, you may put parts of this concern into all three buckets.

You have **direct** control over reading about birth, knowing your choices and articulating them.

You have **indirect** control over whether the medical professionals who care for you read and listen to your choices.

Then it's probable you have **no** control if the baby needs to be delivered in a totally different way for safety reasons.

When you've separated out your concerns pause there. We will expand on this in a moment.

How do you feel now, I wonder?

You may continue to feel relief after this step. When we are overwhelmed things can all clump together, like one massive mess of concerns. Separating things out can, in itself, bring clarity and relief to some.

Step three: Take back control

So we've captured our concerns and begun to separate them out into different levels of control.

Now we are now going to turn that level of control into a prioritized plan of action.

 Take a moment

Look at your list again. For now just focus on the points that have 'D' written by them.

Choose the top two or three priorities – assuming you have a list long enough for this.

A 'priority' might be because it's the most pressing, important or time bound. Alternatively it might simply be because it's a quick win and getting it off your mind will feel good.

For each priority simply choose the first action you need to take. Write it down and put a timeframe against it.

For example, if you have a direct concern that you need to decide how to use your 'Keep in Touch' (KIT) days effectively, then your first action might be to find out exactly what the expectations, allocation and rules around KIT days actually are. To do this, you might decide to make a call to the HR department today.

Slowly begin to develop a list of *small* actions, and of timeframes against them.

For each action, check in with yourself how likely you think it is you will actually do it. If it helps, give it a number on a scale of 1–10 where 1 is 'not at all' and 10 is 'definitely'.

Actions that score under a 7 are unlikely to happen. So for these things break them down just a little further. Make them smaller, easier, and more tangible.

Next turn your attention to the points on your list that have an 'I' written by them. Repeat, by choosing your top two or three priorities. This time separate out the bit you *can* do something about from the bit that requires another person. Once again, determine the first action and put a timeframe around it.

For example, if your indirect control concern is to help recruit your maternity cover, then your first step might be to put aside an hour to review your job description to make sure it reflects what you know you do on a daily basis.

If even this sounds too big to do – then break it down further. For example – step one might be to take 15 minutes to look though the system to find your latest job description.

Once again, pull this together to add to your practical action list.

Now look at your list of actions. How do you feel looking at this? Notice any changes?

The power in this process lies in turning overwhelming worries into small practical actions. We are aiming to move our attention away from the things we can't do anything about onto the things we can.

We all feel better when we think we are 'winning' don't we? Working like mad and feeling like we are 'losing' is totally rubbish.

Finally, let's turn our attention to the points on your original list which you put an 'N' by, as we still need to address these points.

The 'no control' bucket is a little different from the first two, as there won't be any clear practical actions to take.

With the items here, we need to alter the way these concerns are *seen*. We focus on something we term **reframing**.

Cognitive reframing

I was super upset this morning at 7:47am.

At 7:55am I was feeling sad that the morning had been stressful, and that there had been conflict between us.

By 11:50am I was glad it had happened because we'd talked at the gate before going into school. We had accepted that we were late but were no longer concerned about this. We'd hugged, and reminded ourselves that we love each other, and that it's OK that we wind each other up sometimes. It's kind of our job, as a family. We'd smiled about how important it was to be extra brilliant in the remaining minutes of the music class.

Another notch on our belts, another deepening of our family dynamic. We had **reframed** the morning's events.

Cognitive reframing is a technique used in therapy and coaching. It focuses on slightly shifting a person's mindset – usually on something they are finding hard or troubling – with the aim of helping them access a different perspective on it.

For example, if your boss makes critical comments about a piece of work you have completed, you could feel resentful or stressed in response, leading you to a perspective that you're not very good, and believing your boss knows it.

If you were to reframe this, you might add in some different thoughts relating to how supportive your boss normally is, and the good levels of insight they are often able to offer. This could lead to you feeling grateful and more hopeful, holding the view that your work might be even better and more successful because of your boss's input.

This is what we mean when we talk about reframing and it's particularly powerful when we are caught up in negative or unhelpful thought patterns.

The process of reframing isn't about changing the reality of what might happen, but about changing the way we are *viewing* it.

A frequent example I experience in maternity coaching centres on the birth of the child. It's very common for an expectant mother to be worried about the safe arrival of their baby, despite already doing everything that sits within their control.

One way of reframing this could be for the woman to reassure herself that the medical professionals in the room will have the best interests of them and their baby at heart. They will be using their knowledge, skills and training to ensure they deliver the baby to its mother in the safest way possible.

This changes nothing about the reality of the situation but can offer comfort.

Let's have a go at reframing some of your points now.

 Take a moment

Take just one thing for now that has an 'N' by it on your list.

First, we must accept this is a reality and bear the uncomfortable feeling this might present. This could feel similar to the kind of irritation you feel when you find yourself stuck in traffic.

Take a moment to breathe deeply if this is unpleasant and settle with the reality. Some clients find this very easy; for others it requires a few moments of reflection.

Once you feel a little 'acceptance' kicking in, try asking yourself some – or all – of these questions.

- If your closest friend was experiencing this, what would your advice be to them?
- What's the worst that could happen in this situation, and how would you respond to that?
- What's the best thing that could happen in this situation, how would you respond to that?
- What strengths do you have that could help you to navigate this situation?
- When have you handled something like this before, what helped you to do it well?
- Who will be on your side to help you through this situation?
- Who do you want on your side to help you through this situation?
- How likely is it that what you expect will actually happen?

Then finally – knowing this – I wonder if you can view your concern differently. Think back to what I did with my experiences this morning.

Once you've done this, go back to your original concern. How do you feel about it now?

Repeat this process for other points in your 'No Control' bucket.

How do you feel now? As always, take a moment to notice if anything has shifted. All the time we are increasing awareness.

The shift we experience when we reframe changes absolutely *nothing* about the reality of our situation. However it can change absolutely *everything* about the way we feel about it.

This – in my mind – is invaluable.

So there you have it. When we feel 'full up' – tip your concerns out onto a piece of paper. Get them 'out' as opposed to holding them 'in'.

Turn your attention to the things you *can* do something about and develop small, practical actions to take. Then focus on the things you have no control over and work on the way you are viewing them.

This is one effective way to move from feeling overwhelmed to a place with a greater sense of control.

Things change by the moment

I want to reassure you that experiences of worry, overwhelm and control are all part of being human. I was really hyper this morning, worries tumbling out of me. Now, I feel much more balanced again.

Different days in our lives, at different points in our days and at different minutes within our hours we are all shifting.

Sometimes we feel OK, and sometimes we don't.

Sometimes we feel in control, and sometimes we don't.

During the parental transition we can often feel full of concerns and with good reason. The changes taking place are significant. They matter greatly, and it can feel like the stakes are very high.

I believe it's important to accept these feelings and to try not to fight them. In doing so, we can acknowledge and begin to deal with them.

When you feel 'full up', focus on the things you can control as opposed to the things you can't. It will help you to take that next step, and to keep putting one foot forward.

It's clear to see from the work we've done in this chapter how much a working mother has to navigate. Competing demands, needs, feelings and expectations.

Which is why I recommend you focus on one step at a time, and with kindness to yourself along the way.

Part two
Strategies for
taking care
of yourself

5
Self-care

'I just need a moment to think!'

A re you taking care of *yourself?*
When my son was born, he was tiny: healthy and full term but tiny. My partner had to race to the shops after he'd been born as the 'new baby' clothes were so massive he needed 'tiny baby' ones instead.

The reason he was so tiny was down to me.

Ashamed though I am to say it (as I'd wanted my baby at that stage in my life so much) I'd not made me – or us – a priority. I'd been under so much pressure in the last trimester that I'd failed to eat and sleep properly.

There were reasons for this. We knew we were going to need to move house a few weeks after my due date, my partner was in a very stressful year of his work, and I was busy getting ready to take six weeks off from a job that already consumed me.

Then my beautiful – but tiny – baby arrived.

Over the days it seemed he got smaller and smaller. He 'fell off' the bottom of the 'percentile charts'. Yep. We'd go to have him weighed and they couldn't mark his weight in the little red book we were supposed to track things in, because he was smaller than the lowest number on the chart. Lower than the 0.4th percentile – meaning that he was smaller than 99.6% of baby boys of the same age.

This again was down to me; I hadn't learned.

I will be forever grateful to the community midwife who helped me to realize it. She taught me some important things, which could be important for you too.

Let me tell you about Gloria.

Gloria

The reputation of the community midwife team in the centre I was allocated to in North London wasn't that great. So you can imagine how delighted I was when I personally found an incredible bunch of professionals working there. One of them in particular turned out to be my own personal guardian. I will *never* forget her.

Gloria was a straight-talking big-hearted woman, who I first met when she came to visit me in the week I was back home from hospital after my child was born.

It was a Friday, and after checking and weighing him, she sat me down on the sofa and gave me the following clear advice.

'Rachel, over the weekend you are required to do only this. You must sit on this sofa, eat pizza, and feed your baby. That's it. Nothing more. I will come back on Monday, and we will see if there's progress. If you get bored of pizza, eat something else. As long as it's full of calories and you are eating *a lot* of it.'

I've never eaten so much.

On Monday Gloria returned, hooked the baby up to the scales, smiled and said, 'Well done, you've just kept both of you out of hospital.'

As the weeks passed, I visited Gloria in the clinic on a weekly basis. My son's weight – although improving – was still low and progress was slow. The 2nd percentile most definitely nowhere to be seen.

One day she gave me a surprise visit at home. As I went to give her the baby to weigh, she declined to take him.

'No', she said, 'I don't need to see or talk about your lovely boy. He's going to be fine. I want to talk about *you*.'

After lots of tears and conversation, Gloria's point was loud and clear: 'Your baby will be fine, when *you* are fine.'

It wasn't instant, or easy. But over the weeks and months ahead Gloria helped me to see how essential it was to put myself first. If doing this 'just for me' was personally too much of a stretch, then doing it 'for my child' definitely struck a chord.

I hope Gloria knows how truly special she is.

Bottom of the pile

It's not uncommon for clients who have recently become mothers to come into coaching talking about all the different things they have on their minds. Responsibilities to people, to places, to tasks.

Often, after drawing out everything the woman feels responsible for, I am struck by the omission of one thing.

Herself.

Scanning through the points raised in our discussion, I'm frequently unable to find anything about *her*.

'And where are *you* in all of this?' I might ask to a confused looking face. 'What about *you*? I notice you don't seem to feature at all.'

Self-care

Self-care: The practice of taking an active role in one's own wellbeing and happiness

In the decades I've been working as a coach, I've seen huge changes in the volume and usage of these three words: 'self-care', 'wellbeing' and 'happiness'.

There is a lot of information, many products and much dialogue around to help us to 'take care' of ourselves. But how good are you really on a practical, day-to-day basis? Especially during the tough times when you might feel out of balance and under pressure.

In my experience, we're not always brilliant. And, it seems, many of us are struggling.

According to research by the Royal College of Psychiatrists in 2016, approximately 68% of women and 57% of men with mental health problems are parents. The most common problems experienced during and after birth are anxiety, depression and post-traumatic stress disorder.

So what can we do to counteract this?

There are common areas wellbeing and health experts agree are important to focus on. You may have come across these in one form or another before. They are:

- being physically active;
- sleeping well;
- eating well;
- connecting with others; and
- being mindful in the present moment.

Let's take each point one at a time, to ensure we are clear about why it's considered so important to our wellbeing, then I'll offer you the opportunity to do something to reflect for yourself.

Being physically active

It's clearly evidenced that exercise and being active are good for our mental health. Outside of the specific guidelines, the rule of thumb is that it's important you find the activity that is right for you.

Personally I love Pilates and feel that wild horses would struggle to keep me away. The gym on the other hand makes me feel a bit uncomfortable. Exercise is such a personal choice, but something that's important for all of us.

Research also suggests that being outside with nature is good for emotional regulation, so a walk in the park with your baby in the pushchair could be brilliantly beneficial for you.

Sleeping well

Again there are lots of guidelines about the length and quality of sleep we need in order to function well.

This in itself can feel incredibly hard if you're heavily pregnant or have babies and children in the house. When I was first a parent, I completely understood why sleep deprivation was used as a form of torture. It's horrendous, isn't it?

Even with a baby in the house, there are some general guidelines that are still relevant. For example, developing a wind-down routine, avoiding caffeine or alcohol before bed and minimizing screen use.

My partner and I used to do 'shifts' in the night to allow us both to get some sleep. I've heard of other parents doing 'one night on and one night off'. Sleeping when the baby sleeps is also commonly recommended.

Eating well

What we put into our bodies and how that makes us feel is another area steeped in evidence-based research. You will know there's a clear link between what we eat, and how we feel both mentally and physically.

Eating a balanced diet undoubtedly has a positive effect.

Interestingly, there's research not just on *what* to eat but *how* to eat that's very useful.

For example, eating with other people is known to improve our feelings of connection and strengthen relationships, which are important factors in our wellbeing.

For parents of young children this is often a really challenging area to navigate. Hardly any time, maybe limited money and little energy can make it hard to focus on healthy eating.

People often talk about planning and batch cooking as ways to minimize some of the barriers. I'm lucky in that I live with a guy who is an amazing cook. The kitchen is his happy place. I'm very pleased it is.

Gloria was very happy about this too.

Connecting with others

Humans are pack animals, bound by a need to interact and connect with others. It is known that small positive interactions with others lift our mood and sense of wellbeing significantly.

Building connections and relationships provides us with people to talk to, people to listen and to feel understood by.

It's common for clients to talk about how little they've seen of friends since they became a parent, how they've stopped doing things with others that they used to value. Childcare, energy and time are all understandable reasons.

However, as with all these self-care points, doing a little of this can make a massive difference. Planning in advance that one night off, even if it's months away, or making the effort to have a coffee with someone just to say hi and be together will enable you to reap some rewards.

Technology has done wonderful things to improve our feeling of connectedness, but try not to rely on this alone. Nothing quite compares to being physically present with someone who matters to us. It may take a little more planning and time, but it's likely to be worth it.

Being mindful in the present moment

You are probably aware of the principle of 'mindfulness'. It's a state of awareness where our focus is on what is happening at any given moment in time. Not on what just happened, or what might happen, but on what is happening *right now* inside our minds and bodies.

I'll be truthful here. I find this hard. Not the principle – I get the principle. But the reality of it in day-to-day life I find hard. I have a busy brain, usually thinking about things, about opportunities and possibilities. I'm getting better and better though as the years of practice pass. I believe it's a skill, which can be developed through focus.

Clients often find their coaching time enables them to be present and describe it as a chance to 'step off the treadmill'. For most working parents the treadmill is fast, relentless and can feel as though it's never ending.

So how can working mothers build mindfulness into their lives?

From my observations, much of it is to do with routine. Finding the 'thing' that works for you, then sticking to it. Prioritizing yourself in your list of countless other priorities.

Some women I know choose to meditate at a regular time each day. They may use an app to help them.

Some women choose to regularly take part in an activity such as yoga or Pilates.

Some women paint, some women run, and some simply sit and have a cup of tea and take the moment to reflect.

Whatever it is that you need, the advice is to set aside clear time for yourself to simply be present. In this moment, focusing on what is happening inside and outside of you has the potential to energize and balance you. This will enable you to start again from a slightly different (hopefully stronger) place.

Maybe you could treat yourself to a little bit of mindful time right now, by conducting this 'Take a moment' activity, which comes in two parts.

 Take a moment

Part 1: Write down the following list, allowing space between each point.

- Being physically active
- Sleeping well
- Eating well
- Connecting with others
- Being mindful in the present moment

Then give each point a number on a scale of 1–10 where 1 is not at all good and 10 is great.

For example, I might score myself a 7 on being physically active as I'm not perfect but OK at it, and a 3 on being mindful in the present as I find it hard to do.

Once you've given it a number based on your current situation, go back through the list and give it a second number. This one represents where you would *like* it to be. For example, I'd like to move to an 8 on the physically active scale and to a 7 on the mindfulness scale.

The numbers you have written against each point represent the shift you'd like to make in each area.

You may find in some instances you've given the same number. For example, if you've given yourself an 8 for eating well, and you're happy with this, you may simply want to maintain this 8.

You might like to draw it out like the Figure 1 graph:

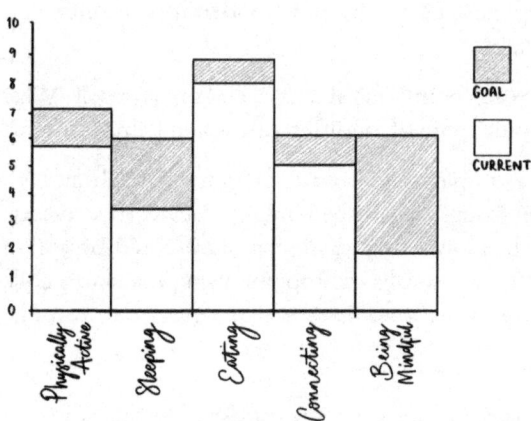

Figure 1: Self-care analysis

What do you notice when you reflect on yours?

It's common to find that there are good things already in place in your routine. This is great. Recognize it and value it.

It's also common for there to be aspects of self-care that we are either ignoring or not fully valuing.

Self-care as we know is multifaceted, so consciously building activities into aspects of our routines brings us reward.

There are amazing resources available to help you develop in these areas. I've added some into the 'Further reading' section at the end of the book.

You might want to view some of these before completing part 2 of the activity. Or, if you've already got ideas to capture, feel free to get started now.

Part 2: The final thing I'd like to ask you to do is this.

Look back over the information you gained from completing Part 1; it's time to identify the shifts you'd like to make.

Take each point, one at a time, and ask yourself 'What will I be doing more of, or differently, when I am at this number?'

For example, if you want to move the 'physically active' scale from 7 to 8, you might decide this means being sure to move every single day. This could be a 20-minute walk between calls or stopping using the car to collect the children from school and walking every day instead.

Small, simple things.

Brainstorm your ideas against each of your points.

Once you've done this, have a look at all your ideas. Choose the ones you think are realistic and doable. Actions that you will take because you *want* to, not because you *think you should*.

Highlight the points on your list that you consider your priority, and determine when you will do that action next, and how you will make sure it happens.

For example, tomorrow while the baby sleeps I will go for a walk in the park. Or, tonight I will walk to collect the children as opposed to driving.

If you find it hard to make the action tangible, break it down step by step until you are clear about what you can committed to doing.

Small, simple, things.

If you commit to your actions and make them happen, you will increase your levels of self-care and wellbeing for certain.

However, we all know that sometimes what we *intend* to do can be different from what we actually end up doing. And sometimes this is down to our **habits**.

Helpful and unhelpful habits

Habit: An automatic reaction to a specific situation

Although I'm crystal clear that it's good for me to pick the children up from school each day on foot as opposed to in the car, I have a sneaky habit that often prevents me from doing it.

I leave it too late to walk. It's as simple – and complicated – as that.

I have a habit of doing 'one last email, call or message' too many, which leaves me tight on time and then stuck with no option to walk. The kids would be waiting outside the closed doors of afterschool club if I did. And I doubt they'd be very happy with me.

So, the habit is the thing that gets in the way, and the habit belongs to me. Which in theory, at least, means I can do something about it.

Habits, though, are tricky little things.

We know that habits are often formed to help us get our needs met in day-to-day life. Often, they are formed subconsciously, which means we may not even know we have them. They become a kind of knee-jerk reaction.

Habits can sometimes be very efficient. They don't require any thought or conscious effort. The seemingly 'just happen'. For example, checking the door is locked before going to bed.

But sometimes they are a pain, and sometimes they don't help us. For example, leaving unwashed cups out on the windowsill to be found days later.

What habits do you have I wonder that might be impacting your levels of self-care? And are they helpful to you or not? Probably a mix.

I recommend you take a few minutes to simply reflect on the 'Take a moment' text.

 Take a moment

In the previous exercise, you developed a list of priority actions, which you'd like to take to support your ability to care for yourself.

For each of the priorities you identified, what habits do you have that will help or hinder their execution?

If you aren't sure, maybe ask your partner, friends, family as they may be able to notice your habits sooner than you do.

Once you'd identified your habits, take a moment to pat yourself on the back. Now we have this awareness, we can do something about changing any unhelpful ones.

Obviously, we want to keep the helpful habits but alter the unhelpful ones.

The good news is that unhelpful habits *can* be adjusted and replaced. Although it's not always easy. Here's how we do it.

1. Identify the habit

You may be able to identify it yourself or, if not, you can ask others. (If you conducted the previous exercise, you've already done this stage!)

2. Reflect on the context

Ask yourself when your habit is playing up. What are you doing? Where are you? See if a pattern starts to emerge.

3. Disrupt the habit

For example, if you are sitting in a particular chair each time you reach for the chocolate instead of your healthy food, then move chairs. Move room. Go for a bath. It doesn't matter; just do something differently.

4. Try something new

Replace your habit with something different. With something that is simple and small.

For example, I have a bad habit of overthinking at the end of the day. It manifests as talking to myself about lots of things at once. I especially do this when I'm really tired. Here it can be hard to control my head. When this happens, I know I need to go to sleep. So I take a bath and go to bed. In the morning, it's often better.

5. Be patient

You will need to practise and keep going while your new habits embed. During this time, please try to be kind to yourself as sometimes you'll manage something new, and other times you might not. Remember, changing behaviour is a process.

You might want to take the unhelpful habits you've been identifying as you go through the upcoming hours and days of your life, and see if you can use these five points to try to change a few things.

Habits don't shift overnight; they take time. If you have a blip, just notice it and try again the next time. It's OK. We are not looking for perfection, but the gradual and effective change of unhelpful habits to helpful ones.

The wheels

I think I'm such a passionate advocate of self-care because I personally find it challenging to do at times. I did before I became a mother, but this increased once I had a child to put first.

However, I do know that if the 'wheels' were to fall off me, they'd fall off a lot of other things too.

This could be the same for you.

You may be lucky enough to have your own Gloria. I truly hope so. I also hope the messages in this chapter go some way to reminding you of just how important you are to so many people and things around you.

Gloria wanted me to be healthy. She also wanted me to be really *happy*. On the inside. And sometimes that's down to taking one simple step at a time, along with a pinch of kindness to ourselves.

So you – and I – both know the value of self-care and in this chapter we've thought practically about how to do this as a working mother.

But it requires discipline. We're working parents, and taking care of ourselves can be very challenging with so many responsibilities surrounding us.

The next strategy I want to share will help you with this. It will help to keep you protected when the headwinds come. Because there will be headwinds. And you're going to need to be well-boundaried.

6
Boundaries

'This isn't quite working for me'

How many people – or things – do you reckon need you at this stage in your life?

In working motherhood everything can feel up for grabs. Your body, your time, your focus, your energy. You are in demand, you are needed.

Your child needs you.
Your partner needs you.
Your friends might need you.
Your wider family might need you.
Your work needs you.
Your line manager probably needs you.
Your colleagues might need you.

This is not to mention the bits of life admin that need you, the voicemail messages that need you, the emails that need you too.

Phew. Exhausting.

And most likely somewhere in the middle of this – being pulled from pillar to post – is *you*.

Sound familiar?

My head used to vibrate. Seriously, it used to feel like my brain was fidgeting inside my skull.

I recall a conversation when someone in my support network expressed concern when I said my head was 'humming' a lot of the time. She sensibly suggested I talk to the doctor in case something was wrong.

But I knew that the cause of it was because I never, *ever* stopped. From the moment something (or someone) broke my sleep, to the moment I rested my head on the pillow again.

It was constant relentless bombardment of noise, information, requests, demands and activity. Some of this external to myself, and some from my own internal voice.

The buzzing in my head was real, and physical. And it was the sound of my complete lack of **personal boundaries**.

At this time I was being pulled from pillar to post because I was allowing myself to be. I was saying 'yes' to anything and everything because I was exhausted, overwhelmed and had no idea what was and wasn't significant.

Reading this I wonder if it's striking any chords?

In complete contrast, there have been times in my life where my boundaries have been clear, communicated and respected. These times leave me feeling free, strong but protected.

Again, I suspect this is true for you.

So let's look at boundaries together. This will enable us to acknowledge the times they are working well, and to change the times when they aren't.

Boundaries

Boundary: A line that marks the limits of an area

What do you think about the definition above, within the context of being needed by lots of other people and things?

Whether you find boundaries easy or challenging, let's take a moment to settle our thoughts on this topic, as there's typically something all of us can learn through pause and reflection. Especially during the motherhood transition, as the volume of moving parts means boundaries need to be frequently reassessed.

Let's start at the beginning. What's the *purpose* of a boundary?

I believe boundaries have a two-fold purpose: to keep things out; and to keep things safe within.

Boundaries represent the rules or limits we set for ourselves, and subsequently for people or things that interact with us.

For example, you may have a boundary that says 'I'm not checking emails after 7pm at night', which is the permission you give yourself to switch off your laptop or work phone at that time.

Or, you may have a boundary that says 'Saturday morning is my one hour of exercise time', which gives you permission to say 'no' to anything that tries to get in the way of it.

There are different types of boundaries. Researchers suggest that there are several different categories that boundaries fall into, and here are a few of the common ones that crop up in maternity coaching.

Emotional

These are boundaries we set that relate to our feelings.

For example, if we feel uncomfortable travelling into the office at 37 weeks pregnant, we may set a boundary by getting agreement to work from home.

Intellectual

These are boundaries we set that relate to our views, thoughts, and opinions.

For example, if we find ourselves with an antenatal teacher who has very set and different views on parenting, we may choose to find a more like-minded teacher to work with.

Physical

These are the boundaries we set that relate to our physical and personal space.

For example, we may insist on an hour alone for a coffee without the baby once a week, just so we can stretch our arms, and be alone for a while.

Time related

These are boundaries we set to protect the focus and use of our time.

For example, if while off on maternity leave, we are requested to attend a few meetings, we may set a boundary that says we agree, but not for the first X number of weeks.

If you have time now, try to reflect more deeply on these areas by completing the 'Take a moment' task.

 Take a moment

Write down the following, leaving a little space between each bullet point, as you'll write in this gap later:

- Emotional – Home
- Emotional – Work

- Intellectual – Home
- Intellectual – Work
- Physical – Home
- Physical – Work
- Time – Home
- Time – Work

Give each of these points a number using a scale of 1–10 (1 being very easy, and 10 being very difficult).

Arrive at the number by asking yourself: 'How easy do I find it to set effective boundaries for myself in this aspect of my life?'

For example, you may find it very difficult to set time-related boundaries at home and give it a 7. But you find doing this at work much easier, so you might give it a 3.

There is no right or wrong; use the scale and be honest with yourself.

When you have done, this reflect on your responses. What do you notice?

I asked a friend who is a working mother to do this activity, and her list looked like this.

Emotional – Home	6
Emotional – Work	4
Intellectual – Home	2
Intellectual – Work	1
Physical – Home	7
Physical – Work	2
Time – Home	8
Time – Work	6

Quite a mix of numbers.

I asked her what she made of her responses, and she said this.

'I always find it difficult to give my own personal feelings the space and focus they deserve. I wasn't really brought up in a family that talked about their feelings, especially difficult ones, so I guess I'm not used to it.'

She went on. 'I feel confident about my views and opinions. I'm employed as a specialist, and I have always had quite strong certainty in my views – and am used to people expecting to hear them.

'The physical one is interesting, as I've noticed a massive difference here since having a child. We physically live in a space where there's no distinction between where adults hang out and where children do, so the lines here are definitely very blurred. I also always seem to have a child hanging off my shoulder or around my feet, trying to kick me, or asking for a hug.

'Work is different. I'm very private, have my own office space and don't really invite any physical interactions with people. I don't think I'm particularly a huggy-person.'

Finally, relating to the time scores she said, 'There's just never enough of this in any aspect of my life. In truth, I think I'm rarely where I'm "supposed to be" or focusing on what I'm "supposed to be" focusing on. There's just too much to do, and it's always so conflicting. I try to put aside time for me, but it always gets swallowed up.'

Wow. These scores are telling her quite a lot, aren't they? Especially about her **beliefs**.

Beliefs

Let's take a moment to explore the principles behind our beliefs, because we know that the beliefs we hold impact what we say and do.

For example, if a woman believes she is wrong to say 'I need an hour to myself now' then she's undermining a need she has and is less likely to ask for that time. In contrast, if she believes she has a right to an hour of space, she's showing an increased sense of self-worth and is much more likely to say 'No, I'm taking this time for me now'.

Interestingly, this process usually ends up confirming the original belief. For example, if I believe I have the right to an hour to myself, ask for it and get it, then I confirm I was right to ask. If I don't believe I have that right and don't ask, then I don't get it – confirming there was probably no point in asking anyway.

If a visual is helpful to you, then take a look at Figure 2.

Figure 2: Beliefs impact

When we think of it like this, we can clearly see the impact of the **belief** that we start with.

And this is really helpful, because when we can identify an underpinning belief, we can understand the impact it has on what happens next.

Underpinning beliefs

Let's go back to my friend, use her examples and look at what they are telling us about her underpinning beliefs.

'I always find it difficult to give my own personal feelings the space and focus they deserve. I wasn't really brought up in a family that talked about their feelings, especially difficult ones, so I guess I'm not used to it.'

Beliefs: I find it difficult to give my own feelings space and focus

My own feelings deserve more space and focus than they get

I'm not used to talking about my feelings, especially difficult ones

'I feel confident about my views and opinions. I'm employed as a specialist, and I have always had quite strong certainty in my views – and am used to people expecting to hear them.'

Beliefs: I am confident in my views and opinions

I am employed as a specialist

I am strong and certain in my views

I assume people expect to hear my views

'The physical one is interesting, as I've noticed a massive difference here since having a child. We physically live in a space where there's no distinction between where adults hang out and where children do, so the lines here are definitely very blurred. I also always seem to have a child hanging off my shoulder or around my feet, trying to kick me, or asking for a hug. Work is different. I'm very private, have my own office space and don't really

invite any physical interactions with people. I don't think I'm particularly a huggy-person.'

Beliefs:
Having a child has changed my view of physical space

Our living space doesn't easily separate adults and children

There's always a child physically in need of me when I'm at home

I'm allowed and given private space at work

I do not invite physical interactions with people at work

I'm not viewed as being physically interactive at work

'There's just never enough of this in any aspect of my life. In truth, I think I'm rarely where I'm "supposed to be" or focusing on what I'm "supposed to be" focusing on. There's just too much to do, and it's always so conflicting. I try to put aside time for me, but it always gets swallowed up.'

Beliefs:
There's not enough time in my life to do what I need to

I'm not doing what I am supposed to be doing

There's too much to do

The things I need to do are in conflict

Time for me always gets swallowed up

See all those beliefs? Some you may think are helpful to her. And some not. But what we know for sure is that they are *all* influential.

If you completed the previous 'Take a moment' exercise, here is the follow-on task.

Take a moment

Go back to your list of scores. For each one ask yourself why you scored it that way. Just the same as I did with my friend.

Capture your responses.

Once you have done this, return to your responses, and ask yourself what they are telling you about your **beliefs**?

Take a moment to capture your thoughts.

When you look at your beliefs you may find, too, that some help you more than others.

I, for example, hold a particularly unhelpful belief that sounds like 'I can rest when everything is done'. And it drives not only me but also my family, round the bend. It's not helpful, as it's unlikely 'everything' will ever be done and it's not really true, as I could choose to relax more frequently than I do.

So I could – should I choose to – *challenge* this belief. I could ask if it's one I really want to keep or not. If it were helpful and true I might want to hold onto it. But it's not, so maybe I could choose to ditch it instead.

Let's have a go with the beliefs you are holding. Here's your extension of the exercise you've been working on.

 Take a moment

Grab the latest version of your list you've been adding to.

For each belief, ask yourself whether is it helpful – or useful – for you to hold that belief?

> If it is, write a 'K' for 'keep' by it.
>
> If it isn't, write a 'D' for 'ditch' by it.
>
> If it is, in some part, but not the exact way you have it, write an 'R' for 'reframe' by it.
>
> How does this make you feel when you look at this list?

You'll recall in chapter 4 on control, we talked about letting go and reframing. It might help you to quickly revisit that information now, as the same principle applies here.

Using the reframing process allows us to slowly challenge our beliefs, enabling us to let go of the unhelpful ones, and develop a list of new, useful and helpful beliefs.

When I asked my friend to do this, she decided to keep the following helpful beliefs.

- My own feelings deserve more space and focus than they get.
- I am confident in my views and opinions.
- I am employed as a specialist.
- I am strong and certain in my views.
- I assume people expect to hear my views.
- I'm allowed and given private space at work.

She decided to ditch, and let go of, these unhelpful beliefs.

- I'm not viewed as being physically interactive at work.
- There's always a child physically in need of me when I'm at home.
- Time for me always gets swallowed up.
- I'm not doing what I am supposed to be doing.
- There's too much to do .
- The things I need to do are in conflict.

And these are the beliefs she wanted to keep but reframe .

- I find it difficult to give my own feelings space and focus.
- I'm not used to talking about my feelings, especially difficult ones.
- Having a child has changed my view of physical space.
- Our living space doesn't easily separate adults and children.
- I do not invite physical interactions with people at work.
- There's not enough time in my life to do what I need to.

This final list, she reframed as follows.

- I have a right to think and feel the way I do.
- It's important for me that I give myself the space to acknowledge my thoughts and feelings.
- I can ask for space and time to allow myself to think and feel.
- I can articulate my thoughts and feelings when I need to, when I've had time to reflect upon them.
- I have a right to personal physical space, and it's essential for my mental wellbeing.
- A grown-up space, free from toys and children, is essential for me to allow myself to think and feel, no matter how small it is.
- It's absolutely fine that I do not invite physical interactions at work.
- There will never be enough time to get everything done; it's all about the choices I make at any given point.

Interesting, isn't it?

My friend took an interesting set of actions because of this insight.

She developed a phrase that she began to use to help her to say, 'I need a moment to reflect on how I feel about this'.

She created a small space in the corner of her bedroom, with a chair positioned so she could look out of the window. She bought a nice new cushion and a candle, and this became her place to retreat to when she needed her space.

Together, as a family, they bought a set of containers to keep the toys in, and developed a new rule that toys were all put away at the end of the day so that the shared space could become a little more 'grown-up' in the evenings.

Finally, she started to learn about choices, and priorities, reading and working on her mindset to help her to determine which priority was in her focus at any given time. This one continues to be a challenge as she's a busy lady, but she's making great progress for sure.

My friend – was setting new **boundaries**.

 Take a moment

Look back at your own 'keep, ditch and reframe' list that you created earlier.

Work through it bit by bit, just like my friend did. What does it tell you about the boundaries *you* need to move, strengthen or put in place?

Identify what needs to happen and who you need to involve.

Then step back and reflect on how this makes you feel.

A lot better, I hope.

The link between our beliefs and behaviour is clear to see. If we are connected to a belief and it really serves us, then our behaviour will allow us to clearly communicate this to others.

They then see the boundary we have in place and the reasoning behind it.

This doesn't automatically mean everyone will adhere to it. Other people and life events may still try to break your boundary wall down. It's likely that at times you will self-sabotage it too.

When this happens, don't get frustrated, but reconnect with your underpinning belief, and use this to reassert the importance of your boundary to yourself and to others.

Remember, it's there to keep you safe, well and happy. It's a form of self-respect.

In the next part of this book, I aim to deepen this principle of self-respect, and really put you at the centre of our thinking. When we become parents, it can feel like we both gain – and lose – parts of ourselves. Sometimes this can leave us questioning who we really are.

So our next set of strategies focus on reconnecting you with your sense of self.

Part three
Strategies for reconnecting with yourself

7
Values

'It just seems like the right thing to do'

Writing this, I have a very specific conversation with a client in mind.

We were sitting in a space near King's Cross (London), exploring how she wanted to negotiate her return to work. Her daughter was four months old, and she was getting ready to begin her conversations with her employer. She was clear that she wanted to be physically back in the office less than she had been before her maternity leave. With the option to work from home sometimes.

This was pre-Covid 19 and negotiating things like flexible working hours or working from home days was incredibly challenging for new mothers. That this has (to some extent) changed seems to me to be one of the more positive things to come out of this time.

The coaching session began in quite a practical way, with paper, pens and sticky notes, as together we were exploring her options. Based on her answers to things like 'What does a good balance look like for you?' we aimed to find her a Plan A, and then a Plan B to help her to agree a return-to-work pattern that worked for everyone.

To begin with, I wanted to help her see *all* her options – even the ones that wouldn't make the cut. I wanted her to explore all the variables and for us to draw out the uncomfortable ones as well as those more ideal.

Working through the process, it was interesting to see just how instinctively she'd react. Within a split second, she'd offer a 'can't think of anything worse' response, or a 'that would be great' reply.

Asking her to articulate *why* – so I could really understand – was much more difficult for her. 'I don't really know Rachel, it just feels… right.'

It just 'feels right'

I believe this phrase is an important one to consider when working with women in the maternity transition. This 'gut' reaction – which draws on weeks, months, years and decades of experience, knowledge, and data – tells us so much.

When something feels 'right' to me, my heart physically unclenches. Which I guess is good for my heart.

I asked my client what she meant when she said, 'it just feels… right'.

'Well, it feels right to read a story to my baby at the end of the day, and to do bath and bedtime.'

'Every day?' I asked.

'No, not every day, but some days. At least two or three in the working week.'

'Why does it feel "right" to do this, do you think?'

'Because it's one of the ways I feel really connected to my child. And being connected is important to me.'

'That's interesting. What does "being connected" mean to you?'

She replied: 'To be connected is to be present in the moment with someone, so they know they matter to you, and that you care about them. It's about sharing an important moment in time together.'

Aah! So there we have it. My client was starting to articulate what would really make her Plan A and Plan B work. It wasn't so much to do with the hours, or days, but to do with an agreed, workable plan that would enable her to share what she considered 'important moments in time' with her daughter.

'Being connected' is a **value** of hers. Understanding and working with our values, when making important life choices and decisions is very, very important.

Let's look at why.

Our values

Human Values: A timeless set of guiding principles

Human values are considered to be our own, personal set of guidelines.

I like to imagine they are like a big strong bubble around us. Everything that comes in through the bubble gets filtered by our values, as does everything that goes out.

The things we *see* other people do, and what we *hear* them say.

The things *we* do and say.

This shows their power, as our values can arguably influence everything to a greater or lesser extent.

When we know our values and can articulate them, we are able to see the impact they have on so much – not least our level of happiness.

As a brief aside, if 'happiness' is a topic you are interested in reading about more widely, there's been a lot of brilliant research taking place over recent decades in this space. The type of work is commonly known as the field of **Positive Psychology**. The focus, in general, is on looking at what works well in people, and how to maximize that. In contrast to the more traditional deficit model of what isn't working, and how to 'fix' it.

I've put some great recommendations for you about this field of psychology in the 'Further reading' section if you'd like to find out more.

For my client, negotiating an agreement in line with her value of 'being connected' was going to be key to making sure it was one that made her happy.

So how attuned are *you* to your values?

If you don't have a clue, then no need for concern as we are going to work through a process of identifying them. We will work with any existing knowledge to gain deeper insight and cement your understanding.

Once identified, we will explore how we can use these to navigate complex situations and find solutions that work for you.

Clarifying your values

Over recent decades researchers have identified processes to help individuals discover the values that are important to them.

Taking the time to identify your values will be an incredibly powerful exercise for you to do. It can help you to develop a set of criteria against which to make important choices.

You'll find a structured activity in the following 'Take a moment' section to help you to do just this. It might be something you choose to do in a couple of 'sittings'. You could make a start, then pause and let it settle, come back and review – and so on. Each time, your thoughts will become clearer and more refined.

 Take a moment

In the back of this book you will find a comprehensive list of core human values (see Appendix B).

Read this list, highlighting the ones that jump off the page as having 'meaning' for you. The ones you personally really relate to.

For example, I might choose 'honesty', 'integrity' or 'tolerance'. But personally, I may not choose 'ambition', 'adventure' or 'fun'.

As you are highlighting the words, please try to avoid overthinking it. Trust your instinct. There is no right or wrong here. Every value has a place. Please avoid thinking about 'how it might sound' to others. That matters not.

If you value 'status', for example, that is fine. Or if you value 'kindness', that is fine too.

Once you have done this, you are likely to still have a very long list of highlighted words. It's expected.

Take the list of words you have highlighted (discarding the unhighlighted) and repeat the process again, looking at which of the words really jump off the page for you.

Repeat, and repeat this process until you get to the stage where you have something more like 10 or 12 words left. Fewer is fine too.

We will work with these chosen values shortly, so put them to one side just for now.

It has taken me time to refine my own understanding of my personal values. And now, I choose to keep a list of mine on my phone and refer to them from time to time to see how I feel, whether anything has changed focus or developed.

I also use them as a check list. If I've had a good day, I see what my values tell me about why. If I've had a bad day, the answer about 'why' can always be found in this list too.

One of my kids this weekend kind of, sort of, tried to ask me if he could buy a Pokémon toy he'd had his eye on. We went around so many houses before he spat it out. I found myself beginning to get a bit impatient. Not because of what he was asking for, but because I value courage, and somewhere deep inside I wanted him to have the courage to simply say 'Mum, I want to spend my pocket money'.

Clearly this tells us much more about me, than him, but that's the point of our values. They guide *our* thinking and responses. They guide how we act and how we behave. And understanding this is important. I found myself able to say 'Hey, just tell me what you'd like to do', which he did. And got the shock of his life when I simply said 'Sure'.

He's now the proud owner of *another* 'plush Pokémon' and happier because of it. He's also now a step closer to knowing that he can be clear and honest with his mum. And I'm even happier because of that.

Once you've identified your values, as you walk through your daily life refer to your list, checking how you think it may or may not be influencing you at this point in time.

The process of values identification is a very significant (and my clients tell me rewarding) one. So don't feel like you must rush or force it. There are no prizes for getting 'there' quickly. Enjoy working with the thoughts you've begun to identify in the activity above.

Articulating your values

Identifying values is one thing. Knowing that 'honesty', for example, is important to you can be of use in itself.

However, to benefit more deeply from this insight, we really need to take it a stage further. We need to be able to **articulate** them.

This is when our understanding can become effective and powerful.

Remember that values are considered to be 'subjective'. They belong to the person themselves, and their meaning is personal. As a coach I've probably heard in excess of 50 people talk about 'fairness' as an important value, but when questioned about what it means, each individual articulates it in their own personal way.

For example, I've heard it described by one client as:

- trying to be 'wide' in what you hear;
- taking on board different perspectives;
- thinking about other people.

… and another client as:

- giving everyone the same level of attention;
- appreciating that people express themselves differently;
- not judging people.

Interesting isn't it?

All that really matters is what the value means in the eyes, mind and heart of the person who holds it.

When we understand the true meaning of our values, we can help other people to understand it too, we can use it to help inform our choices, our decisions and many other things.

So let's work with your values and articulate what they mean to you. This is where we find out what *you* think is important.

Here's an extension of the previous exercise.

 Take a moment

Take the list of values you settled earlier. At this stage, the number matters not.

We are going to work on articulating and distilling these to really capture their true meaning. It's probable we will end up at the stage where you have around seven core values.

Take each of your words one by one and articulate what it means to you. Not the dictionary definition, or what you think other people consider it to mean. We aren't interested in anyone other than you, and your view.

With clients I always suggest they simply start with bullet points, writing their thoughts down. It can help to use words such as 'doing', 'being', 'having', 'knowing', as these help you really embody the meaning. Here's an example of some from the client I mentioned earlier.

Warm-heartedness

- Looking past barriers, positions and judgements
- Seeing others and being seen as individual yet connected
- Having a genuine curiosity and like for people

Dignity

- Being able to look people in the eye
- Making decisions that are not intended to wrong other people
- Taking actions that are honest
- Not putting your needs ahead of other people's

Have a go with each of the words you have on your list. As you do this you may find some similarities emerge and that you are talking about the same thing across two different words. If this is the case, then choose the one that most reflects your thoughts and discard the other.

This is how you will further refine your list and get to the point where you settle on the core ones. Typically, as I've mentioned, it's around seven that we settle on.

When you have done this, take some time to settle with your descriptions. Maybe ponder them, using the following questions to instigate thought.

- How do these values play out when you are having a 'good day'? When was the last time you experienced this?
- How do these values play out when you are having a 'bad day'? Again, when was the last time you experienced this?
- What people do you have in your life (work and home) who display these values? How do you feel when you are with these people?
- What people do you have in your life who don't display these values? Now how do your interactions with them make you feel?
- What kinds of activities or tasks do you engage in which are in line with these values? How do you feel when undertaking these tasks?

- What kinds of activities or tasks do you engage in which are not in line with these values? How do you feel when you are undertaking these tasks?

Please don't force your responses to these. Go gently over the hours and days being curious and seeing what you unearth.

You may find you have a few things confirmed or that you find new answers instead. All are useful. All are valid.

Once you've started, you may find that your individual values begin to fall into groups. For example, you may have some that are people focused, some that are communication focused, or some that are task or activity focused. Or you may not. That's fine too.

If I think about my values, I have a few that are focused on learning, such as growth and challenge. I also have a few grouped around interpersonal communication such as non-judgement and curiosity.

Having worked on this with clients for many years, some people seem to also find what I call a 'golden thread' that weaves through all of them. Just like a seam.

Even after 20 years of exploring this myself I'm still working on articulating mine. It's linked with open-mindedness, tolerance, and non-judgement of self and others. But as you can see, I'm hardly slick at describing it, so work is still there to be done!

Using your values

Knowing and being close to our values – being able to articulate them is a wonderful thing. It grows further in impact though, when we look at how we *use* this understanding and insight.

Below are three key ways I believe they can be of incredible use.

1. Making choices that work for you

In the maternity transition working women are faced with a constant barrage of choices and decisions to make. As I've mentioned previously these are often around big things to do with children, home and work.

Often, women arrive in coaching sessions conflicted. Their employer wants something, their family has a view, or society has set expectations. Working out what 'you' want can be really helpful in all that noise.

One way to do this is by cross-referencing your choices against your values. Your answers will often be found in your descriptions.

For example, one of my clients held 'availability' as an important value. One day she was wrestling with whether it was time for her to do an MBA. She appeared to be really struggling, so I asked to see if her values could help her to gain new insight. She looked at them, and immediately responded with 'It's not the right time just now, is it?'

I asked why. She said: 'Because I won't be available for my daughter as she moves to secondary school. Next year will be different, but this September, she's going to need me, and I want to be available for her.'

So she delayed her course, started the year after and felt a heap better about it in the meantime. What's important though is that it was *her* choice, and in this situation led in part by her core values.

What choices are you facing now? Refer to what you know about your values, as maybe these could help you make a decision that feels 'right' for you.

2. Communicating accurately

Your values can also help you to be way more accurate when communicating with other people.

Let's use my client from the start of this chapter as our example here. We know that 'being connected' was significant to her. She'd told us so, and for her this meant being there for her daughter at 'important moments in time'.

As part of her conversation with her employer about her return to work she went in with a well-considered Plan A.

As they were exploring what could work, her employer asked her questions about length of days and the flexibility she would be able to have. My client told me that she used her knowledge of her values to articulate clearly and openly what would and wouldn't work for her. She described how useful it was to be able to say: 'I'm very happy to work some longer days and can see the importance of that. What's important to me though is that this isn't every single night. I need to have time to connect with my child several nights a week at the end of the day and bedtime. If I prioritize this on agreed days, then the rest of the week I can work longer for sure.'

I asked her what difference she felt this had made, and she described it as much less combative, more authentic than if she had gone in with a more rigid message to her employer.

Next time you are faced with communicating what's important to you – refer to your values and see if they can offer insight into ways to share your message clearly. It's often not the 'what' but the 'why' underpinning it that really matters. And this is the language led by our values.

3. Increasing your levels of happiness and wellbeing

I expect it's easy for you to see the link here now that we have explored what our values are and how they impact our happiness levels.

Usually employers want happy employees, children want happy mothers, and as working women, we strive to simply be 'happy' too.

Your 'North Star'

In the transition into working motherhood, there are so many significant choices and decisions to be made. These choices are often complex and can involve lots of stakeholders with their own valid needs and views.

When to work, how to work, who will care for your child, when to look after yourself, when to take care of friends. The list is long and important.

Navigating this will always be challenging, but using your values as the 'North Star' to guide your thinking, aid your communication and support *your* happiness is a really smart thing to do.

The North Star is a powerful anchor. And we need to move on your momentum with this, continuing to work on strengthening and connecting you to your core. At a time of life that can sometimes feel draining, we are going to turn our attention to your energizers. Focusing on what *gives* you strength.

And oh my days, I often plead for someone to 'give me strength… !!'

8
Strengths

'Oh no, I can't bear the thought of doing that again!'

The best 'feedback' I ever received was from my two-year-old in the Tate Modern art gallery one afternoon when, mid-meltdown, he loudly proclaimed he wanted another mummy because I wasn't 'very good'. We looked around to see if there were any takers.

Whether it's willingly or reluctantly, formally or informally, we can often find ourselves on the receiving end of 'feedback'.

There are lots of things over my career and life I've realized I'm not 'very good' at. Slowing down, packing to go on holiday or being brave enough to state my own needs. These are sometimes positioned as my 'weaknesses'.

In contrast, I'm told there are things I'm 'good' at. Talking, making birthday cakes and coaching (phew!). People tell me these are my 'strengths'.

Now, let's get this out right at the beginning of the chapter. The things you're good at aren't necessarily your **strengths**.

There you go, I've said it.

In fact, sometimes the things you're good at can leave you feeling anything *but* strong.

My draining strength

I'm ridiculously good at organizing things.

I don't know why. I can just see, plan and sort things. According to some people I make it look effortless.

Early in my career this meant that 'organizing things' often came my way. I just seemed to attract this kind of work.

At one stage I had management graduates to organize on a retailers' training programme. Individual needs, learning needs, business needs. So many 'needs' to coordinate.

And I could do it. Somehow, I could navigate it. No matter how high the volume or intensity of the content.

But shhhh. Do you want to know a secret?

I absolutely hated it, and I *dreaded* it.

Why? Because I'd rather stick pins in my eyes than organize stuff.

Organizing stuff often makes me feel anxious, fretful, confused, conflicted and many different emotions in between. I can feel my flesh physically change temperature and my mood shift when I have to 'get organizing'. Even the thought drains me.

For me, this was intensified by 'motherhood'. *So many things* to organize – a constant stream of stuff. School bags, activities, play dates, shopping, spellings, reading and on, and on, and on, and on, and still on.

Sometimes, this feels like it might consume me. And yet. Despite how it makes me feel. I'm really, really good at it. I can even make it look easy.

Dispelling the myth

Ask many people about their strengths and they will talk about what they consider themselves to be 'good at'.

Ask people what they are **energized** by, and you might be surprised at the difference in their responses.

But why is this relevant to working parents?

This is why.

My friend Olivia is a happy working mother. She's often considered to be a 'powerhouse' of a woman. People see her as a great partner, fun friend, brilliant professional and present mum. And you know what – she is all of these things. Sure, she has other parts to her as well, but these descriptions of her are visible a heap of the time. She works super hard, but she's usually very content, satisfied and happy.

Over the years I've watched her, talked to her, and tried to understand the answer to how she can be like this.

It's not because her life is perfect, that's impossible, and hers definitely isn't. It doesn't appear to be because she's got a particularly sunny disposition. In contrast she's very realistic in her thinking.

It's not because she's got heaps of cash. In fact, I recall her one day saying, 'I'm spending pretty much all my monthly salary on childcare and it's crippling us, but I'll be damned if I don't have a career – that I've already worked 15 years for – to go back to after having children!'

No, it appears to be something to do with the choices she makes. Where she puts her focus.

I have asked her about this – lots – over time. And have become increasingly clear about the filter she uses for her focus. It's to do with choosing (as much as possible), to do things she is drawn to, the things that *give* her energy and *increase* her happiness.

In essence she exerts all the control she can over **maximizing her energizers and minimizing her drainers**.

What Olivia does – by her own admission without conscious thought – is play to her strengths. Whenever possible.

Unwittingly, she's great evidence of some important underpinning psychological theory.

Character strengths

The area of 'character strengths' is well researched. Well-known names (specifically in the field of Positive Psychology) have turned their focus to understanding and analysing them. Remember, there's additional information on this in the 'Further reading' section, should you be interested in learning more.

There's a shared agreement among these minds that our strengths are innate. Wired in us and beautifully described as natural, energizing capacities that we yearn to use by psychologists Govindji and Linley (2007).

To illustrate this, let me share an example of my own.

If I wake on a Tuesday morning, and a whole day of report reading, form filling lies ahead. Personally I am going to feel drained by the thought of this and exhausted by the end of the day. Likewise, if I am faced with a day without any human interaction, I will be flat and distracted by the end of it.

In contrast – no matter how exhausted I feel at the start of that Tuesday, if I am faced with coaching all day (which is intense) I guarantee you I will be 'high' at the end of it. Why? Because some things drain me, and some things energize me – they literally give me strength.

Doing craft activities with my children energizes me. I love it. Doing music practice drains me. I'm sorry, but it does.

Our strengths are likely to bring together a combination of factors. Our skills, knowledge, and experience for sure, but also our natural talents.

Some researchers suggest that people are *drawn* to things that energize them. I tested this in a business environment with an Exec client of mine. He put a 'project' to his team and asked them to stick their hands up for the bit they were *drawn* towards. Interestingly one person wanted to do the analysis part, another the stakeholder engagement part and so on. We mapped these against what we knew of their energizers and there was a link. Luckily for him, he had a well-balanced team! Of maybe it was design. He's a great leader, so it could very well have been intentional.

So we've got high energy givers, a link with our talents, and a 'magnetic pull' as principles we can use to help us understand your strengths.

Once we know them, we can work on how you can bring these into your life to support your happiness and energy levels. And blimey do we need this during our transition into working motherhood!

Quick note – if you intend to begin this exercise now be aware that in it, I suggest you keep a log of your activities over a period of time. This activity is one to start and to monitor as opposed to being done in a single sitting.

I strongly recommend you take the time to do it though, and it will only need a few minutes from you each day. So it's not an arduous task at all.

 Take a moment

Make a note of a few of the activities you have done so far today. It doesn't matter what they are – big or small, unusual, or mundane.

For example, you might write down 'putting the washing out, reading to the children, logging on to a meeting, going for a walk and calling a friend'.

For each activity, ask yourself the following questions.

- Did you feel energized after doing it? Did you feel a sense of satisfaction?
- Were you good at it – did you demonstrate 'success'?
- Were you drawn towards it? Because you *wanted* to not just because you *had* to?

For the activities you have answered 'yes' to, write them down on your paper under the heading 'things that give me some strength'.

For those you have answered 'no' to, write them down on your paper under the heading 'things that drain me'.

If you can, please repeat this for several days. The more data you collect the deeper the insight for you will be. If you have a great memory (unlike menopausal me!), you can think retrospectively too – what happened yesterday and the day before for example.

> You will end up with a list of activities that you believe *give* you strength and a list of things that you feel *drain* you of energy.
>
> I wonder how this feels now you look at it?

When I conducted the first part of the activity above, my initial list looked like this:

Things that energize me

- Colouring quietly by myself
- Coaching
- Pilates
- Talking to my supervisor (who is kind of like my own coach)
- Building the business strategy with my business partner
- Having time to reflect in a calm coffee shop
- Reading a challenging article and taking something from it

Things that drain me

- Reviewing the accountant's email
- Doing chores – sorting the washing, tidying up, speaking to utility providers
- Having the 'same' chat with someone about the 'same' thing that doesn't seem to go anywhere
- Having to sort out the car insurance
- Answering emails
- Getting my 'snail like' children out of the house for school

I'd love to be able to see what yours looks like. How balanced it is, whether one list is noticeably longer than the other. Just doing this part of the activity can offer you useful insight.

But now, if you're ready to move on, let's extend our thinking and move onto part two.

 Take a moment

Once you're happy you've enough to work with, take half an hour or so, to see what your data tells you. Ask yourself:

- What has been confirmed for you?
- What is new, does anything surprise you?
- What patterns or themes can you see? For example there may be patterns around things you do by yourself or with others. Things you do outside or inside.
- What – in summary – would you say are your key strengths and your key drainers based on what you know so far?

What do you notice, and how does looking at your notes make you feel?

My own personal reflection reads something like this, and I find it very reassuring as it helps me to confirm what I think I know about myself. It also serves as a good reminder too for when things go off track (which they inevitably do!).

My reflections on my energizers:

- Overcoming challenging problems, and having to think creatively to find solutions
- Interacting with others frequently, especially through exploratory discussion, learning together
- Learning something new, whether through doing, reading, talking
- Having variety in my life and tasks
- Challenging myself physically and mentally to achieve things I didn't know I could

- Taking time by myself to be present – doing crafts with my hands, walking, or listening to music

My reflections on my drainers:

- Reading and evaluating documents or articles with lots of words on them
- Sorting and organizing lots of things in one go, especially if they sit at different levels (some urgent, some important, some neither, some both, some simple, some difficult, etc.)
- Thankless household chores that keep multiplying without getting anywhere
- Boring conversations or interactions that achieve nothing, seem repetitive and don't go anywhere

I can see patterns around movement and progress. I can see patterns around learning and challenge. I can see patterns around both interaction and reflection – and the choice I need to have available to me as to which I need at any given moment in time.

This is something I've come to appreciate more recently. Maybe it's age, maybe it's the busy home and work life I lead, but my need for solitude and calm is something I think I've ignored in the past. And yet it's a great source of energy for me.

When I suggest clients undertake this activity, it's interesting to see their responses afterwards as it varies.

How are you feeling?

You might be feeling reassured. What you thought you knew is indeed what you have found out.

You might feel relieved, because it explains a lot about *why* you are feeling the way you are.

Or maybe you feel concerned, because it helps you to see how much of the activity you engage with drains you, and how little energy you currently derive in the day-to-day.

Whatever your response, it's important we acknowledge it and use it. *Everything* can be helpful for us.

Having taken the time to identify your strengths, your next action is to think about how you maximize them.

A balancing act

Let's get real here and talk about balance.

Why?

Because as much I might like to, I can't eradicate the forever multiplying household chores that drain me of every bit of energy I have. I've tried very hard, and they are still there winking at me. I have to do some of these things. That's 'grown up life'.

I must do the washing, and I must put (at least some of) it away. It's important I read the insurance document to check it's accurate, and that I book the car in for a service. It's part of my job as a responsible adult.

On a work front it's important I log my practice hours, write proposals, and run evaluation checks. It's part of my professional standards and responsibility.

For reasons like this, we are not usually able to remove all the drainers, but what we can do is control the volume and frequency with which we engage with some of them. We can also make sure that we consciously pepper things into our day that energize us, to balance some of the other things out.

And that's the important factor, and where the significant shift can be made.

My friend Olivia, who I mentioned earlier is smart at ensuring she spends as much time as possible doing the things that energize her, and as little as possible doing the things that don't.

She's clever at ensuring every day she balances out the negatives with the positives. Some things take her energy, other things fill her up. In balance, this means she's never 'running dry'.

I asked her recently what she was up to at the weekend. She'd previously told me she was shattered, so I fully expected her to say 'nothing'. Instead she was meeting up with some friends for food after the children were in bed. She said this made her feel so good, and really reenergized her and set her up for the week ahead again. It wouldn't work for me, but it does for her, and she knows it. Which is exactly the point.

If you are completing the activities in this chapter, here's your final part now. As you do this, I'd like you to have the word 'balance' in your mind.

 Take a moment

Reflect upon your day today. Whether it is extending itself out in front of you, or whether it is ending.

What does today's balance look like in 'Energizers vs Drainers' terms?

Mine is about 80% drainers so far, and 20% energizers. I'm at about 1pm in the afternoon, so this makes me think about what I've got on for the rest for the day. I need to get my balance in check. I'm prompted to think I'll go for a walk before I collect the children tonight and listen to a podcast I've been wanting to listen to as I do.

Now that automatically makes me feel better. I'm giving myself the chance to increase my energy levels and draw strength from the activities I'm engaging with.

So, what does your balance look like? And what does your response suggest you need to focus on?

Determine what you need, and make it happen. Even if it's something small it will make a difference to you, I promise. As usual, I want you to find a realistic action and commit to it.

During the transition into being a working mother, it can often feel like we are bereft of choices. So many responsibilities, and little choice about what to engage with, and what not to.

However, if you consider what we have been talking about in this chapter so far, I hope you will see that we can challenge this notion. Sure, we can't let go of everything that drains us, but we can choose to balance it out with the good stuff. That's the bit that is in our control.

And in doing this we can embrace the *whole* us.

Your authentic expression

One final point from me about the wonderful – almost nutritional value of strengths – before we move on.

Earlier I mentioned that our strengths are, as Govindji and Linley (2007) suggest, natural capacities that we long to put to use; these enable not only authentic expression but they energise us too.

I'd like to highlight the word **authentic** and bring your attention to it because it's important.

Definitions articulate being authentic as meaning things such as 'being real and true', or 'genuine, not a copy'. A significant message for everyone in so many aspects of life. I believe it's particularly important for working mothers.

Why? Because there's no 'one way' to do any of this parenting, working thing. There's '*your* way'. And this chapter – along with the ones before and the ones still to come – is working towards helping you clarify, articulate, and take authentic actions.

As a coach, my aim here is to empower you to understand the core of you, and to use this knowledge to make *your* best choices.

In 2000 a brilliant article on authenticity was written, which ended with the powerful suggestion that we should be ourselves more, but with skill (Goffee and Jones, 2000).

And that's what we are slowly doing. Reconnecting you with your core self. Clarifying and focusing this understanding so that you can use it skilfully to enable you to be that brilliant working mother you *know* you really are.

I feel a surge of energy writing this, and we are going to surf this wave and take ourselves straight into the next chapter. Our focus is on motivation – which is all about our energy and drive towards something. It's about movement with purpose and intent.

And motivation will provide you with increased energy and focus – which all working mothers benefit from – and increased happiness.

Which working mothers deserve.

9
Motivation

'It feels so good!'

LBK

LBK.

Life. Before. Kids.

Aah the hazy, lazy days of LBK.

Those *wonderful* days.

Those days of... those days of... of....

Wait...

What were those the days of?!

I had 20 adult years of LBK. Yet I can remember so little of it. My 'Life Before Kids' memories are vague to say the very least.

Yet I do recall being so driven. I travelled, I studied, I partied, I learned, I built relationships, I built a business, and I had fun.

Lots of happy fun. I had ambition and I was most definitely motivated.

Then I became a parent, and my life changed. So did my motivation.

I had responsibilities. I had big responsibilities. I had expectations, and other people had expectations. I had a new baby, and I had so much love to give, and wanted to take the very best care of him I could.

And with his arrival, my motivation felt like it had shifted *forever*.

Motivation

Motivation: The reason behind a willingness to do something

Let's start by understanding the core principles of motivation before we think about how motivated you are.

I began my career working with leaders, coaching and supporting their development. In leadership work there are some core subjects that underpin most things. One of them is the topic of motivation.

It's looked at from multiple angles such as 'how to motivate people to do their job' and 'how to motivate others to follow you' through to 'how to motivate yourself to deal with everything that comes your way during the day'.

The principles of human motivation are some of the most well considered, studied across centuries of research that looks at the subject from so many different angles. Reward, challenge, needs, equity to name just a few.

I believe the people who have researched this behaviour have brilliant minds. They are insightful, and they have all looked from different but useful angles. I've added some suggestions in the 'Further reading' section if you'd like to understand more about motivation as a topic.

Motivational principles weave through my coaching practice like a golden thread. And in conversation, there's something I, as a coach, am often looking out for.

I'm looking for something I call **'the want'**.

I need to understand what a person wants, and importantly *why* they want it. I need to understand if there are barriers preventing a person satisfying their 'want', so that we can explore ways to overcome them.

And why do I need this? Because I serve the needs of my clients, and if they can articulate this to me, they are articulating it to themselves too. Then we have connection, and with connection we have increased motivation.

When motivated, we have a desire for change that comes from deep inside. Which in turn encourages us to *act*.

What's your 'want'?

Life either has – or is – changing for you. Life changes when we become parents.

And this in turn changes your motivations. It changes what you are being driven by, and what you are heading towards. It changes what you want. Maybe not everything you want, but some things for sure.

What mattered to you before, may – or may not – matter so much now. You might have loved nights out with friends but would now rather be at home with your family. You might have thought you were driven by the next big promotion, or getting the 'top job', but you may no longer be so bothered about this. Or in contrast you might be even *more* bothered about this.

You might have thought city living was definitely for you, and now you strive to move back to where you spent your own childhood. Or you might be driven by a need for more money as life has got a whole load more expensive.

I share these as examples only – although they are common. The arrival of a child can shift many component parts of our lives, challenging what we thought we knew, what we thought mattered to us.

I wonder how your motivation is shifting, during this phase of your life? Do you know? The 'Take a moment' task may help you to answer this.

 Take a moment

We all have different individual parts to our lives. Most common are ones like these:

1. Significant other (relationship)
2. Child(ren)
3. Family (wider than the above)
4. Friends
5. Physical health (fitness, exercise, food)
6. Psychological health (mental wellbeing)
7. Learning or growth
8. Fun (hobbies, holidays)
9. Short-term financial health (money)
10. Longer-term financial health (security)
11. Home environment
12. Work/career short term
13. Work/career long term
14. Community (wider contribution, volunteering)

Now, this list isn't exhaustive, but it's a great starting point.

Take a moment to write down the categories that form the different parts of *your* life using the list to help you. Feel free to add or take away as you wish.

Some people like to add things like 'spirituality' for example. Others may take away short- and long-term financial health and put it all under 'money' instead.

Decide *your* list. Then write them down on a piece of paper simply putting a number by each one. As I have done above.

Using the scale of 1–10, where 1 is extremely dissatisfied and 10 is extremely satisfied, put a number against each of your components signifying the extent to which you are **satisfied** with it.

For example, I might put a 6 against physical health as it's OK but could be better, and an 8 against work as it's clear, I'm focused, know what I'm working towards and so on.

Looking at your current satisfaction levels of your life ask yourself:

- What are you already doing in each of those aspects which means you've given it the score you have?

For example, even if you've scored a 2 in one area, what's happening that means it's not a 1? Capture the good stuff and be sure to note it down.

Once you've done this reflect on the following questions.

- Which aspects have scored highly?
- Which have received a low score?
- Which scores are you happy – or OK – with?
- Which scores are you not happy – or OK – with?

Simply note your reflections. We are gathering information bit by bit and will build on this shortly.

When we look at our life as a whole – particularly when it has been fundamentally changed with something as significant as the arrival of a child – it can be anything from enlightening to sobering.

Maybe your responses make you feel happy or maybe not. Maybe they throw up lots of questions, or in contrast provide you with some answers.

And we use this insight to propel us forward.

Your future focus

So far, we've begun to develop an understanding of the present. Let's now turn our focus to the future and look at what you are working towards.

Here's the next thing for you to do.

 Take a moment

Return to your numbered list. This time give it the score you'd like to see if 12 months from now.

For example, I might like to move physical health from a 6 to an 8, and I might like to maintain work as an 8.

Once you've done this for all of the different aspects ask yourself the following:

- Which aspects require the most significant change?
- Which aspects require little – or no – change?

What do you notice at this point? Just draw these observations out and reflect.

When I work with clients to create an objective perspective of where they are now and where they are wanting to move towards, it is typically extremely powerful. Being able to take the 'whole' and break it down can offer rich and valuable insight.

I often ask clients questions such as these.

- What did you already know that you've had confirmed here?
- What's surprising to you, and why?
- What (if anything) unsettles or concerns you?
- What (if anything) reassures you, or makes you happy?
- What (if any) themes can you see? Might there be more progress to make at work than at home, or maybe things that relate to you directly need more work than things that involve others.
- If you were to prioritize areas in terms of the most pressing, significant, or maybe urgent, which would you say require your attention first?

I believe that through this level of reflection you will find not only insight but reassurance. The kind offered by clarity and connection. When our thoughts are clear and we can 'see' what matters to us, we typically find a sense of connection towards making something happen.

We find our **motivation**.

Moving forward

Our final step is to join the dots using the insight you've gained so far from this chapter.

Take a moment

Look at your notes. For each aspect of your life, look at the shift you want to make, and ask yourself what will be different when you've made that shift.

For example, I have moved physical health from a 6 to an 8. If I ask myself what will be different when I am at an 8, I might answer:

- Increasing Pilates to 3 x per week
- Making sure I move away from my desk every single day for at least 30 mins
- Planning meals on a weekend for the week ahead
- Batch cooking on a Sunday

For maintaining work at an 8, I might answer:

- Sticking to my 2 x coaching days, 2 x writing days and 1 x business development day structure
- Setting all quarterly meetings in advance to ensure they are in and will happen
- Booking in my next professional development course for the autumn so I know my CPD won't go by the wayside.

Move through each of your categories adding to the list all the things you want to do.

Don't filter them in terms of how realistic they are just yet, as we will work more with this list in a moment.

The process outlined supports us in identifying what we could focus on to increase our levels of satisfaction and happiness.

Let me take a moment to share a story with you about how this can look in reality.

A few years ago I worked with a maternity client who had come back into the workplace after the birth of her first child. Sadly, she wasn't in a great place. She found herself pulled between so many conflicting thoughts, feelings, expectations and responsibilities that her motivation was really low.

She was struggling with juggling her work and home responsibilities. She felt financially tied to living in her current home and working at her place of work. But financing a physical or work move seemed impossible. She was having panic attacks with worry, and feeling deeply conflicted about where her life was taking her. Once career driven, she felt a shadow of herself unable to find the energy to even begin to think about what to change. Trapped, I think it's fair to say, with no energy to find a route out.

In about our third conversation, I asked her which part of her life she wanted to see change in first. I went on to suggest we use the principle we've been discussing in this chapter to try to take a step back, hopeful this could help her find insight to drive enough motivation to help her out of her rut.

As she began to separate out and work with the process, you could see the relief begin to show in her body. She started to talk with energy and more clarity than I'd seen in her before – developing a list of possible practical actions to help her to regain a sense of control.

As her list grew, I encouraged her not to worry about 'how' she might make some things happen, but simply to let her thoughts flow and to brainstorm all her ideas. I reassured her we could work with the whole list eventually and determine our starting point.

Once she'd finished, I started to ask her the following.

- Are there any 'quick wins' here for you?
- Which points will provide you with the most immediate relief?

- Which points are the more important for you?
- Are there any points which have a timeframe attached to them?

She chose her priorities. They covered actions relating to self-care, to her ways of working and to her finances. They involved talking to her partner, her own mother and to her boss.

A short while after this third session, she messaged to say secured herself a promotion and moved house. She was more motivated than ever.

 Take a moment

Take your list of possible actions, as it's time to get practical.

Work through the questions below to filter out your top priorities.

- Are there any 'quick wins' here for you?
- Which points will provide you with the most immediate relief?
- Which points are the more important for you?
- Are there any points which have a timeframe attached to them?

It's up to you how many questions you have. Be realistic, though. I'd like you to set yourself up to succeed as opposed to fail.

Motivation breeds motivation, so if you choose a few priorities, be sure to do them, as you'll be more inclined to come back and work on the next ones.

If motivation is about connection and movement from somewhere towards somewhere, I hope by this stage you have more clarity about your current situation, where you are heading and how you get there.

Build on the knowledge you gained from our previous chapter on control and remember to focus on the things you can directly do something about first. As always, if it's too big break it down again and again until it's tangible.

LAK

LAK.

Life. After. Kids.

We are still here. We are still us, riding the waves, facing the headwinds, and chasing our dreams.

The process I outline in this chapter is one you can repeat – not just at this stage of your life, but at many other points. Once the children have arrived through to once they've left home and beyond.

Personally I take the time to do this activity once a year – usually towards the end of it – assessing my current state, and planning my focus for the new year to come. I transfer my actions onto my phone and use them to keep me clear and connected as the months progress. The sense of satisfaction I find when I reflect and see what I've achieved is wonderful. The sense of clarity I gain from connecting with my goals is deeply energizing.

Writing this reminds me that it's nearly my time to do it again. I might grab a coffee after this myself and begin capturing my own reflections. I wonder what they will throw up this time?

Part four
Strategies for working with others

10
Effectiveness

'I just need more time'

Her first meeting was at 9:30am on a windy Monday morning. Easing into the meeting room gratefully clutching a steaming hot coffee, she settled in her seat and took a deep, deep breath. Her working week was just beginning.

Before this, she'd done a few things.

She'd fed a screaming baby at 4:45am and changed a nappy. She'd tried to go back to sleep and failed miserably.

She'd got up and fed the cats, put the washing up away, and put the first load of washing on. She'd put breakfast things out.

She'd had a shower, but before having the chance to get herself dressed, she'd said good morning to her sleepy five-year-old.

She'd picked up the 'now awake again' baby and taken him into her room. She'd got dressed. Well almost. She'd stopped midway to get the five-year-old some clothes out of the wardrobe and ready for school.

She'd continued getting herself dressed until the baby vomited while she was halfway through doing her shirt up, so she'd cleaned that up instead.

She'd responded to the scream from the five-year-old who was now downstairs. He'd dropped milk over the kitchen floor. She'd muttered to herself under her breath.

She'd answered the door *very* enthusiastically to her mother-in-law, given her the baby, the upset five-year-old and the milky floor cloth.

She'd finished getting ready in speed time, kissed everyone goodbye and legged it out of the house as quickly as possible. Only to realize she'd forgotten to explain a few things to her mother-in-law.

After doing this, she'd hugged her wonderful but complex brood goodbye, and once again stepped out of the house.

She'd breathed deeply on the way to the station. Enjoying the wind in her hair and the air in her lungs.

But she'd forgotten there were works on the line, so she'd got the 'slow bus to nowhere' instead. Fortunately, she'd taken this unexpected opportunity to respond to her emails, and to do her prep for her first meeting of the week.

She'd got into work only a 'little late' and realized she'd never managed to do her shirt buttons up.

She'd finished getting dressed, made a coffee and stepped into her first meeting of the week…

Familiar anyone?

Most working mothers I know are bright, capable women, who understand the importance of being efficient. But I also know that this can be easier said than done when faced with the relentless stream of needs, demands and expectations like those outlined above.

Let's unpick some of this next.

The wonderfully harsh truth

I've developed a new equation I want to share with you.

Working Mother + Stuff to Do = *Never* Enough Time

Let's face it. There will never be enough time to do everything that's expected or required of you.

No time management matrix, no fancy organization method will ever be enough for you to think, do and *be* everything that is required of you.

It's simply not possible. I'm sorry to be the bearer of bad news.

Or *is* it bad news?

If it is, then maybe there's a gift in there for us. Why? Because it means we *must* make a choice about what or who gets our precious attention at any given time.

And we know that with choice comes the opportunity for freedom and empowerment.

In this chapter, I want to look at the concept and structure of time. Because contrary to what we may assume, I don't think it's all created equal, and that's very useful for a working parent. Especially when we are choosing what gets our attention with the little time we have.

The quality of time

Time: The indefinite continued progress of existence

Wow that's a good definition isn't it? No mention of 24/7 or the 'structure' of time as we know it.

And aren't our days structured?! Not only into sleeping and waking hours, but into 30-minute meeting slots, one hour TV shows and so on. Add a child or two into the mix and the structure intensifies. Feeding time, nap time, school days, term time and so on.

Even writing this makes me feel slightly caged and diminishes my sense of 'choice'. But this is far from the truth. It may sometimes *feel* that way, but it doesn't have to *be* that way.

Let me show you why.

One of the most obvious ways we structure our 'time' is into **waking and sleeping hours**.

Let's start with the significance of our sleeping hours.

It's widely regarded that we need a certain amount of sleep to be rested and effective. Both lack of, and excessive, sleep can cause problems ranging from depression and problems concentrating, through to changes in our sex drive. Timings seem to vary between research papers, but often seven – eight hours a night crops up as healthy for an adult. However, the amount of time isn't the only important thing. The *quality* is too.

What is generally agreed is that uninterrupted sleep is best of all. It would appear we have a few different stages of sleep, which form part of a cycle – from lighter through to the deeper sleep which is considered essential for our brain maintenance and development. Our engagement in 'deep sleep' is the bit that leaves us feeling well slept.

I know, I know. If you are reading this as new parent, you will be thinking 'Exactly! That's why I feel so rotten all the time!'

And yes, it is *exactly* why.

Because your beautiful child interrupts your deep sleep *a lot*. Which can leave you feeling absolutely rubbish at times, and to be effective, we need to be well slept. Constant interruptions just don't work over periods of time.

Now what's particularly interesting, and *much* less talked about, is that we have the **same needs in our waking hours**.

To be effective in our waking hours we also need blocks of uninterrupted *quality* time, to allow us to engage fully at certain tasks. We need this to feel good. The same way we need deep sleep to feel good. Failure to have this in our waking hours leaves us feeling akin to a bad night's sleep. Dreadful.

But our waking hours are much less well explored than our sleeping ones. We don't talk about them with the same level of shared insight at all.

So let's talk about it together now.

Psychological flow

According to Csikszentmihalyi (2013), 'flow' is a state of mind. It is a mental state of immersion, which takes place when we are awake. The equivalent of deep sleep.

For example, have you ever been so focused on something that you lost track of time? If so, it's probable you were in this deep flow-like state. You may even have forgotten to take care of your basic needs in this time, like drinking the coffee you made, or even going to the toilet.

When you finished the activity and came up for air, not only might you have noticed that time has whizzed by, but also you may have felt a great sense of achievement, even a whoosh of energy and contentment with the output of your efforts.

This is the experience of flow.

As work into this deep state of thinking developed it became apparent that there are some external conditions that can help a person to engage at this level.

Common factors that help are thought to be things like:

- giving ourselves a block of time to focus fully on something (around 90 minutes);
- making sure we have no interruptions during this time;
- making sure the activity we are focusing on is a challenge but also achievable; or
- making sure the activity we are engaging in has meaning – something we feel connected to and can see the 'point of'.

These conditions are the waking equivalent of things like having dark curtains and no tech in a bedroom to enable sleep.

Now I don't know about you, but in my two main roles in life – a professional and a mother – I can't think of many opportunities when I get an uninterrupted 90 minutes to focus on something that has meaning and stretch for me. Can you?

And this is *precisely the problem.*

Societally and individually we acknowledge the times when we are deprived of deep sleep during the night. We respect this need and set up structures to satisfy it.

But we don't offer the same level of respect to our waking hours. We rarely – if ever – acknowledge lack of engagement in flow when we are awake.

No wonder many of us are left feeling fraught and exhausted.

So let's use this knowledge to change things for the better.

Shredded time vs flow time

Yesterday I set out hopeful. The day ahead of me only had a couple of meetings planned, the rest of my time was set aside to focus on important things such as reviewing a document and beginning to plan a new project.

Things started going wrong when the doorbell rang. It was my neighbour asking to borrow a garden waste sack. Which turned into a 25-minute chat.

I returned to the written document.

Then my laptop pinged. Darn it! Instinctively I looked at the message. It was booking for a weekend event which was becoming urgent as tickets were going quickly.

I went onto the internet, booked the places, messaged my friend, and returned to the written document.

I re-read the same paragraph I'd already read twice that morning, as I'd forgotten where I was up to.

And so this pattern continued… Until I'd simply run out of time. There was a call scheduled in my diary.

I didn't make it past the first two pages of the written document, and I was nowhere near the project I'd expected to work either. Irritatingly and frustratingly the time had 'vanished'.

Often, I find life is like this. To me, it can feel like a paper shredder. I look out at a stretch of six hours in front of me full of hopes and dreams of what I can achieve, but instead it gets shredded bit by bit into small, unfulfilling moments.

You know that feeling when you walk into work all hopeful on a Monday morning about the week ahead, and you suddenly find yourself at Friday wondering what on earth you've been so busy with for the last five days? Most probably still holding onto Monday's to-do list, which seems only to have multiplied.

Hear that? Yep. That's the sound of time getting shredded.

Now how do you feel at these moments? Pretty rubbish if you're anything like me. Disheartened, tired and heavy.

A bit like you do when you get a broken night's sleep by any chance? Exactly! Because this is what shredding does to us.

And it usually feels overwhelming and exhausting.

So, what can we change?

We can introduce more quality – flow like – time. *That's* what we can do.

I'm not pretending this is easy, but I am saying – for the record – that it's possible. With intention, with boundaries and with self-control.

If I had wanted to boundary my time yesterday, I would have ignored the doorbell. Had I been on a call, I would not have answered the door, because I would consider the call too important. So, I could have offered the same level of respect to the document I was working on too. Maybe even put some headphones on to help me concentrate and to cut out any interruptions.

I would have put my laptop onto 'focus mode'. I'd have switched everything off to remove the 'pings'.

There are many ways in which I could have respected and valued the importance of the work I was doing in those 90 minutes. Sadly, I didn't.

But 'our focus' is exactly that. Ours. Which means we can often choose what gets it and where to put it. And as usual it's about balance, priorities and choice.

So let's work on this now.

Shredded tasks and flow tasks

Let's start by understanding what activities or tasks fall into each group. Because essentially we want shredded tasks being completed in 'shredded time', and flow tasks being engaged with in 'flow time'.

Shredded tasks are also sometimes called 'mechanical tasks'. They are the short, sharp, repetitive tasks that all of us must engage with.

For example, checking emails, sorting the washing, or attending an update meeting. These kinds of tasks are typically transactional and require some, but limited thought.

In contrast, flow tasks are sometimes called 'cognitive tasks'. They are the bigger, more challenging, often meaningful tasks that many of us strive to engage with.

For example, creating a new strategy, shaving five minutes off a 5k running time, or exploring a new book with a young child. These kinds of tasks are typically ones we consider important, and we need to open our minds when engaging with them.

Let's use your day so far to get a deeper sense of this.

 Take a moment

Reflect on your day so far. What things you have done since waking up? Simply go back in your memory and make a list.

Once you've done this, put an S for 'shredded' and F for 'flow' against each one to represent what type of task it was.

When you've done this reflect on what you see. The following prompts could be useful for you.

- What's the overall balance between shredded and flow tasks looking like?
- How did the shredded tasks leave you feeling after you'd done them?
- If you have flow tasks there, how did they leave you feeling after you'd done them?
- Are you happy with your balance, or would you like it to be different?

Add any other reflections that come to mind to your thinking.

Take a moment to reflect on what you see.

I have worked with many people who have gone from having no quality time in their waking hours to finding a great balance that works for them.

Some engage in flow on certain days of the week, others more at weekends or evenings. Everyone has a different structure. The only 'right' is the one that works for you.

One client of mine found her 'right' and it looked a bit like this.

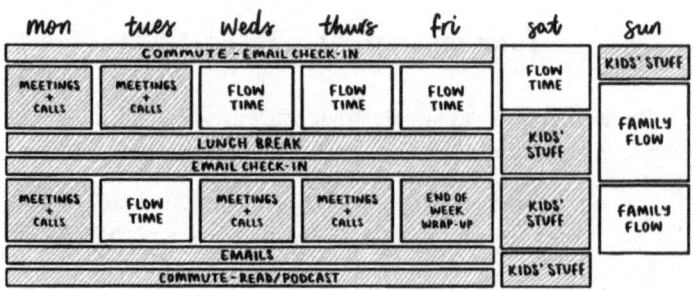

Figure 3: Time map

For her there was an acceptance that Mondays were totally 'shredded', and this helped her to manage her expectations on that day. She stopped starting the week with big expectations and feeling on the 'back foot' by the end of Mondays. Instead, she changed her mindset and accepted that the important stuff usually only got her focus from Tuesday onwards.

She also boundaried her 'flow' time. It kind of became sacred to her – particularly on a Saturday morning – as this was her way to decompress from the week and to ease into the weekend. She began to say 'wild horses' couldn't keep her away from her 9am Saturday spin class.

Now, it's not *always* like you see it in the picture for her. There are days and weeks that mean things change, of course, but this is the point she always tries to come back to. If an email comes in and she sees it needs thoughtful work. She will look at her next available flow opportunity and book it in for then. Responding to the email with: 'Yep, I've got this. I'm going to work on it on Wednesday when I have the opportunity for proper thought, and will get back to you.'

And if her exercise class must move, it moves. But… before simply moving something she now asks herself: 'If this time was important to me, where am I going to engage in this instead? Because clearly, I believe I need it.'

When I have my own balance 'right', I know I feel good and energized. When I don't, I know I feel stretched, drained and out of sync.

What would you like your balance to look like?

The 'Take a moment' that follows may help you to make the shift towards making your use of time better for *you*. It looks at your use of time from a day through to a whole week. It's one for you to play with to make useful, with the time you have available. Read through it, and you'll see what it asks of you.

Take a moment

Part one: Current

Either using one day, a series of days, or a whole week, build a picture of the quality of the time you currently engage in. Is it shredded or is it flow? If it helps, you can use different colours or shading to give you a sense visually, like in the picture above.

Part two: Desired

Once you've completed Part one, take a moment to reflect on what you see. Being really realistic – to set yourself up to succeed as opposed to fail – what would 'better' look like for you?

For example, it might be doing something on a Wednesday night, or Saturday morning like my client. Or it could be moving some team meetings onto the same day.

Part three: Shifts to make

Finally, use the above and ask yourself this question:

- For me to turn my desired time into reality, what are the changes I want to make?

For example, it might be to contact a colleague and ask to move a meeting or to investigate local classes on a Saturday morning and book yourself on one.

Once you've got a list of actions, ask yourself these questions.

- Which are in my direct control (see chapter 5) and my priority? What action do I need to take?

> - Which are in my indirect control and my priority? Who else does this involve? What action do I need to take?
>
> As you work through this process, you will see a list of practical actions begin to form.
>
> Be realistic with your actions; make them small and attainable. Shifting towards one more opportunity to engage in flow per week is great progress. Embed that, then you can always find a way to add a little more.

Personally, I find that it is an ongoing process to find ways to create enough quality time in my days. Especially when there are children involved. Once we get our heads around one routine, something changes and it's all up for grabs again.

The rule of thumb is if you're feeling strung out, like you're running from one thing to the next, or spinning around on a tiny plate, then it's probably a sign you need a little more free-thinking flow time. A very simple question to get into the habit of asking yourself is: 'When will my flow time be today?'

We simply can't be effective without good quality sleep.

We simply can't be effective without engaging in flow.

Being effective

Working Mother + Stuff to Do = Never *Enough Time*

As you have read in this chapter, I believe this to be true. It's all about choice – making choices on what gets your attention and what doesn't. Not right there and then anyway. The baby, or email, might need to wait just for a moment.

It's critical to our ability to be effective.

I am a stronger person when I have slept well *and* when I engage in activities that energize me. And as a stronger person I am better placed to navigate the headwinds that working motherhood puts my way.

I trust that you too can see how these powerful principles could empower you right here, right now.

Remember the lady at the start of this chapter? She's made some changes.

Now she allows herself the privilege of getting dressed in one go. She makes this a priority, and she does it before anything else. She says it helps her to feel a step ahead.

On her way into work she does emails. On her way home she now listens to a podcast to 'zone out and decompress' before returning home.

Every Wednesday morning she has two hours blocked out in her diary. She works from a coffee shop and focuses on one work thing that requires her attention.

And on a Saturday, she's carved out an hour for her exercise.

Simple shifts. Not a massive overhaul, but realistic small things begin with. She will do more when she's ready.

And she's so much happier for it. I hope the strategy in this chapter will make you feel happier and more in control of the choice you are making with your time too.

11
Communication

'There's something I really need to say…'

Ｎone of us operate in isolation.

We interact with other people constantly. Sometimes about simple things, and sometimes about more complex things. Sometimes we agree, and sometimes we don't.

Big life changes, like parenthood, bring so many things into question. Some things solidify in our minds, some things change, and needs can surface that we didn't realize we had before.

As a working parent, there will be lots of this that you need – and want – to communicate to others.

Some of it will be easy to share, but some of it may not be.

Sometimes, it's hard to talk

'How many people did you make cry today mummy?' one of my children inquisitively asked one day while we were walking home from school.

The conversation paused.

I have worked with wonderful women over the course of my career, and almost every single one of them has had a point in our relationship where they have cried. At least once.

As I told my son, Mum doesn't go out to make people cry. I promise. However, I realize I often do.

Why? Because my job is to see and to hear people. My job is to create space for someone to be, to think and to feel. And to create the opportunity for them to talk and be heard.

My job is to offer a space for them to communicate *fully* with another person and in turn I challenge them to communicate fully with *me*.

I'm fundamentally a 'communicator' by profession.

And when the words begin, they often flow. Tumbling out, like a dam has burst and the water clambers in desperation to get out.

I have a client's face in mind as I write this – although she represents many. We had a session a few weeks after she'd returned to work following the birth of her son.

I asked her how she was. She said 'good'. But she didn't look good to me. She looked small, she looked empty, she looked flat. I responded, 'I'm not sure I believe you, are you certain you feel good?'

That was it. She slumped forward and cried...

The art of communicating

To communicate: Giving information, expressing ideas or feelings either verbally or non-verbally

Well this definition makes it all sound so simple, doesn't it? But talking – especially about important things – can be anything *but* simple. Sometimes even working out what information to share, what ideas we have, or feelings we are experiencing can be like climbing an impossibly steep hill.

For a working mother, when everything is topsy-turvy, the ability to be clear enough to communicate can feel really difficult.

The client I've just referred to is a brilliant communicator – articulate and effective. But interestingly, not only had she seemingly lost her ability to communicate, but she also hadn't even realized that talking was something she'd stopped doing.

Her tears were important. They were her way, in that moment, of telling us so many significant things. They were her sign that she *needed* to talk.

I asked her simply: 'If you could say something, to someone, what would you really like to say?' I listened as she talked.

Turns out she had loads to say.

In particular, there was a lot that she wanted to share with her line manager about her unhappiness and her feeling of not 'belonging'. She wanted to tell him how angry she was about how he'd interacted with her over important things during her maternity leave.

She wanted to tell him that she loved her job but felt like she didn't want to do it anymore. Not like this.

She wanted to tell him she was hurt. How could he judge her after all she had done over the years.

She wanted to ask him why he was pretending everything was great, when clearly it was not. For her, and she suspected, for him too.

She wanted to ask him why he'd not yet met with her since she came back, and why he was avoiding talking to her. How dare he not even talk to her about this!

Wait…

'He's not talked to you?' I enquired.

'No, not at all,' she responded crossly.

'Oh, that's interesting. And have you talked to him?'

Pause…

'On man…' she realized, eyes wide open, 'No, not at all.'

'OK, and why not, do you think?'

'I don't know…,' she mumbled. Unconvincingly.

'I wonder if you do. Take a moment to think about it,' I said.

Pause…

'I'm scared. I don't know what I'd say. What if he reacts badly? What if it makes things worse?'

'Yep, That's a real concern for sure. And what if you *don't* start talking. How bad could that get?' I enquired.

'Very… if it stays like this, I'm not sure I can work there for much longer.'

'How much longer would you stay if nothing changes?'

'Truthfully?' She hesitated, as if acknowledging something fully to herself, 'I'm already starting to look for other work.'

'OK, so it sounds like talking could be the *better* of the options then. Talking, maybe before it's too late…' I said, looking at her.

I saw her shoulders ease, her eyes look up, and she took a deeper breath than I suspect she'd taken for a while.

And then, we started planning her conversation. Exploring *what* she wanted to say, and *how* she wanted to say it.

In doing so, she was finding the words, confidence, and motivation to talk.

She went on to have a healthy conversation. Sharing important information she needed to share with the person who needed to hear it.

I'll share more about 'how' we did this in a moment. But before we move on, I'd like to give you the opportunity to check in with anything you might be wanting to say to someone.

 Take a moment

Grab a pen and blank piece of paper.

Imagine there's no risk. I'm going to take it all away. For now, it's just you, your thoughts and piece of paper which no one else needs to even see. Unless you want them to.

What are all the things you'd like to say, if you could? Maybe you're excited and want to share it; maybe you're concerned; maybe you're trying to solve a dilemma you're facing. Maybe you're angry or sad about something. Maybe you're tired, or simply in need of a hug.

Don't overthink it. Don't worry about 'how' you say it, or 'who' you say this to. We will get there eventually. Just get out everything you'd really, really like to be able to say.

This may take you 30 seconds, or you may find that once you start, it flows and flows. Start, and then stop only when finished.

When you've done this, reflect on your words using the prompts that follow.

- How does it feel having got all that 'out'? Better, worse, scary, reassuring? Or something else?
- Who are the people who you feel need to hear this? List them. Don't worry about whether you do, or don't, end up sharing anything. Let's just identify the people for now. For example, a partner, a colleague, your employer.
- Are there any key themes emerging? There may or may not be.

Then, move onto these two questions.

1. What are the risks of saying any of this?
2. What are the risks of **not** saying any of this?

Gather your thoughts and allow time for your brain to process and to reflect.

In this exercise I ask two critical questions at the end.

What are the risks of communicating what's on your mind, and what are the risks of *not* communicating what's on your mind?

In my experience, we are very adept at including the former in our decision making, and much less likely to include the latter.

I asked my client about her view of the risks, and she responded with certainty.

The risks lay in *not* talking.

So with a deep breath, she worked out how to say – what she needed to say – and then she said it.

The heart of the matter

We've just completed one of the most important aspects of the communication process – checking in with how we are feeling and what we are thinking. This is the catalyst for everything that comes after.

Once we acknowledge there's something we want to say – or share – then we move through to a way more practical approach about how to set about *doing* that.

My client knew she needed to share some messages with her boss. When I asked her there was a lot of information, so to remind you of what she said, I've included them here.

- Emotions: she feels unhappy, angry, judged, hurt and sad.
- Experiences: she doesn't feel like she belongs anymore or like the way he interacted with her while she was on leave.
- Views: she loves her job but not the way it currently is and she wants them to be truthful with each other.

She *wants* to talk.

Now what do you think? Should she share all of these points? Or just some? Remember, she'd already decided that sharing none of them was no longer an option for her.

This *is* a real dilemma, isn't it? Her points are potentially important, and useful.

I asked my client: 'Which of all these things is the *most* significant for you?'

She looked at all the things she wanted to say, and her response was clear.

She wanted to tell him that she loved her job but felt like she didn't want to do it anymore. Not like this.

She said some of the points from the past were important, but not nearly as important as working out what happens now moving forward.

This makes sense to me. As we know from our work around control there's nothing we can do about past events. They have happened, and we will have our individual, possibly different, views of them. If we think about now to the future, then we have more control, more influence in determining how things conclude.

 Take a moment

We're building on the previous 'Take a moment', so look at everything you have written down, and do the following.

- Ask yourself: what are the most significant points that you need to share?
- Then identify *who* you need to share this with.

Simply make a note for now.

It takes two

Being clear about what we want to say, and who we want to say it to, is important. But communication is a two-way thing. My client needed to talk to her boss. And her boss would have a view too.

Now, we have another person in the mix.

She wanted to say: 'I love my job. But I don't think I want to do it anymore – at least not like this…'

But what might he want to say?

Put yourself into the shoes of her boss for a moment. How might he feel being on the receiving end of this?

He could feel shocked. He could feel sad. He could feel angry. He could feel attacked. Either way, he's certainly going to have his own view and perspective on the situation.

And this is one of the fundamental challenges of **interpersonal communication**. We have two human beings interacting – often about important things – with their own set of views, experiences and opinions all in the mix. Take a look at Figure 4 for how I like to visualize it.

Figure 4: Interaction cycle – perceived

I say something (verbally or non-verbally) and you respond.

This social interaction is often called a 'transaction' (Berne, 1968) and they can either be 'good' or 'not good' ones. Which we all recognize as the difference between a nice or healthy chat, and a more uncomfortable one.

But we already know from our work in chapter 2 that people are anything but two dimensional. We are made up of loads of things. Our values, our drivers, our beliefs, our hopes... to name but a few. So more accurately, our interactions with others look like those in Figure 5.

Figure 5: Interaction cycle – actual

And it's *exactly this* that can make talking incredibly challenging. Especially when it's about things that are important to us.

Simply 'being human' makes things potentially so much more complicated. And it always leaves me wondering how on earth any of us interact effectively most of the time. There's so much room for misunderstanding, conflicting needs, imperfect messages.

At the heart of interpersonal communication lies one critical message. Once you know what you want to say, put yourself into the other person's shoes, and look at it from their perspective. Use this insight to help you position your message.

My client did this. Based on her knowledge of her boss she thought the following.

- He suspects I'm not 100% happy.
- He knows I've a lot on at home with the new baby.
- He knows things aren't quite right between us.
- He wants to do a good job and hit targets.

- He needs a strong team around him to do this.
- He might be concerned about losing me.

Now this may or may not be accurate, but it is based on what she knows about him.

What do you know about the perspective of the person – or people – you need to talk to? If you've been following the stages of the 'Take a moment' task in this chapter, here's your next part.

 Take a moment

Take your reflections so far.

Now put yourself in the shoes of the person you want to talk to for a moment. Based on what you know of them, what might their perspective be?

Make a note of your thoughts and try to be as objective about it as you possibly can.

What do you notice after doing this?

Let's now think about how we use the insight of perspective to position messages effectively.

'Grown up' communication

Having identified what she really wanted – and needed – to say to her boss, my client had one final bit of thinking to do before acting.

To work out 'how' to say it.

She could say 'I'm so cross with you, I hate my job now, and I can't wait to get out of this dump!' but I doubt many of us would think that this would go down well.

She could say 'I'm so sad, so unhappy, I can't work like this anymore'. Which may well get a different response.

Or... she could say something more like this.

'Look, I love my job. But I'm not sure it's quite working for me, and I wonder if you feel the same way too? Can we talk about it, and share our thoughts so we can see how we might make things better for both of us, and for the wider team?'

Ooh. That might do something interesting don't you think?

Researchers have some shared views about what makes communication successful – especially when it's about something that really matters to us and might be difficult to address. I've recommended some books for you in the 'Further reading' section about this.

In summary, the core principles are:

- stick to the 'here and now' – it's so much easier than rehashing the past;
- try to agree a shared objective – you will probably find that there is some common ground;
- be objective – use facts and avoid judgement wherever you can;
- demonstrate respect – through sharing, questioning to understand and listening;
- express your ownership of thoughts, feelings, and opinions – it's OK to speak 'your truth'; and
- make clear, direct requests – especially about what would make things better for you.

These are effective principles known to enable balanced, grown-up communication and minimize chances of unhelpful conflict.

In a moment I'm going to invite you to plan the conversation you already know you need to have.

To help, I will give you some sample phrases, based on the points you have just read. Use these to help you structure what you want to say.

- The facts of the situation as I see them are...
- I've taken the time to listen to what's important to you, and I ask that you now do the same for me...
- Let's focus our energy on looking forward and finding a solution that suits both of us, shall we?
- What's the most significant factor for you here? What's important to me is...
- From my perspective I think/feel...
- I'd personally like to see X happen...

One of my clients calls these her 'power phrases', as she finds them useful in many different situations.

If you are completing this chapter's 'Take a moment', here's the final piece of the jigsaw for you.

 Take a moment

You know want you want to say, and who you want to say it to. So now we are going to work on *how* you do it.

Use the bullet points listed earlier – the characteristics and the phrases – to help you determine exactly what it is you want to say.

Write the words down, but don't expect it to be perfect first time; you may need a few attempts. That's cool.

Once you've written it out: check it is balanced; check it is fair; and importantly check it is true to what you feel –

to your truth. Even speak it out loud if it helps. Hearing yourself can be very powerful.

Notice how you feel once you've done this.

Clients tell me that they often feel a sense of relief when they have identified what they need to talk to someone about and have actually done it.

Sometimes talking is necessary – and sometimes it's not. But when it is – doing it with truthfulness, with considered thought, and with kind intent is key.

A happy ending

My client talked to her boss who listened. He talked to her, and she listened.

They agreed that things weren't going too well, and they agreed it wasn't sustainable. They agreed they both wanted the same thing, to be happy and successful in their roles. And they agreed they would keep on talking.

Which they did.

A few months after their initial conversation, she left her job.

It was the right decision for her, and her boss agreed. He fully supported her as she found a new role, and she supported him as he found a new person for her role.

She was a happy, good and effective leaver, and will always be remembered as a valued employee.

Part five
Strategies for managing milestones

12
Handing over for maternity leave

'What if they're better than me, what if they're worse?!'

'Boy childcare V8' read an Excel sheet I emailed to my partner one day, along with the message 'please print two copies – one for you and one for the fridge'.

It came a week after V7. And a week before V9.

It detailed what was happening, when, where and who was in charge at all stages of the day and week.

And I thought I was calm about all of this.

When we have a baby, and we hand over to whoever is providing the childcare, we do so with such an astonishing level of care.

I went back to work quite soon after my children's arrival – as I've already mentioned – and I used a whole blend of different childcare support. Each time I left my child, I'd leave an impressive 'handover'. University level in terms of research, detail and robustness.

It read something like this.

8am	Breakfast (incl. full explanation of menu, pots, spoon, cutlery to use)
9am	Clear up and re-bath child to remove breakfast mess from hair, face, toes, etc. (incl. full explanation of water temperature, thermometer to use, soap location, towel location)
9:30am	Playtime! (incl. full explanation of what was on that day, directions, timings, snacks to take, which of the millions of small Tupperware pots to put the snacks in, which bag to pack, what to put in it and where to find it and other essential stuff)
11am	Milk!
12:30pm	Lunch (incl. how to cut the tomatoes up)
2:00pm	Nap time (incl. which lights to have on, room temperature, what to do in extended crying situations, how long to expect nap to last for)
4pm	Playtime!
5:30pm	Teatime
6:15pm	Bath time
6:45pm	Cbeebies
7:00pm	Bedtime (incl. which PJs to wear, creams to use, songs to sing, story to read)

Why did I do this?

I suspect it's to do with the depth of meaning my child has to me, and the importance I knew there was in handing over well.

Important for me, important for him, but important for the person 'taking the reins' too.

Depth of meaning.

Importance for me, for my son and his carer in handing over well.

Let's use this line of thinking and move our attention to 'handing over' at work.

Because in my experience, the baby handover and the work handover have surprising similarities.

'I've *got* to write my handover…!'

This came from the mouth of one soon to be mother. She was at lunchtime on her last day before leaving to have her baby. Her due date was only a week later.

It was accompanied by: '… and I've got an interview for my replacement this afternoon too. It's a been a nightmare finding someone.'

Busy afternoon, I remember thinking.

It turned out she'd 'started' her handover 'ages ago'. By this she meant she'd created a new word document and been punching things into it.

She wanted to use this coaching session to do more thinking about it.

To begin with I asked her how much her work mattered to her, and why.

Turned out she cared about it *a lot*.

It was her income and a big part of the overall household income.

It was part of her identity too. She loved the role she did, was proud of the brand she worked for. She enjoyed getting on the tube each day, grabbing a coffee and listening to some music on the way.

Her work also formed a big part of her motivation. She considered the organization as one really making a difference. She was connected to it at a deep level – the purpose, the values – really feeling like she belonged.

I was struck by the contrast between how much this work meant to her – on so many different levels – and the lack of consideration that had been afforded to handing it over with care.

I'm not judging her at all – I'm just really curious. I know she wanted her job to be well looked after, cared for and ready for her to be picked up when she returned. All in one piece.

So why such little thought about how to make this happen? Sure time was squeezed, but it always is.

I think this was more than finding the 'time' to do it. We find ways to prioritize the things we know are important to us.

It must be to do with how we *view* the work handover. More as an action, as opposed to *why* we take that action.

Because if we think about why we may want to hand over our work well. There are lots of reasons.

What meaning does your work have for you I wonder? I suspect your role means a lot. Maybe in different ways to some I've outlined above, but it *always* has meaning.

And in this meaning you'll find that there's an importance in handing over well. For you, for the team, organization, clients you work with, your child, your household and so on.

Which means it warrants so much more thought than a hastily put together word document.

Let's look more at how to handover effectively when we consider the depth of its meaning.

Your 'work baby'

What state do you want your job to be in when you get pick it up again?

Do you want things to have changed or stayed the same? Are there projects to be completed and monitored that you've already started. Are there things on the horizon to be planned?

It's important to ask these questions. Because *what* you want to come back to, has an important role to play in *how* you hand over.

Let me share an example with you.

My friend Femi is a brilliant woman. A creative thinker with a clear focus on work life balance. When leaving for her second maternity leave, I asked her what she wanted things to be like when she returned. She was clear and responded, 'well maintained'. She wanted things to remain on an even keel, the fundamentals intact and stakeholders happy.

In contrast my client who I mentioned earlier in this chapter was struggling to find a cover she was happy with in part because that individual was taking on her role during an enormously important time. A big new project was coming to fruition that she'd been working on for years. In her words the timing of her pregnancy couldn't have been worse as far as her work was concerned.

Femi was looking for a maintenance plan.

My client was looking for a progressive plan.

Not better, or worse, just different.

What isn't remotely unique though, is the planning that needs to take place for this to be done effectively.

I've broken this planning down into four steps for you, with some activities included. If you are reading this and in the process of thinking about your handover, then I strongly suggest you take the time to go through the steps and activities as thoroughly as possible.

If now isn't your exact handover time, I'd recommend you have a read through, but come back to the activities when your time does arrive.

I also suggest you consider your handover as a series of documents as opposed to one. It's a good idea to begin creating a 'handover file' moving things into it as you work through the process outlined below. This way you gather relevant information bit by bit.

Also – upfront – I **strongly recommend** you begin this whole process a good few months before you leave. It's more effective and less stressful if done gradually over time.

Step one

Ask yourself: What is my role now, and what do I want it to be like when it gets 'handed back'?

When I handed my baby over, my (robust!) instructions were deliberately there to make sure that when I picked him up, he was healthy and as happy as could be. I wanted him returned in broadly the same state as I'd left him.

So this is our starting point (see 'Take a moment'). Let's turn our attention to your role at this very moment in time. We need to begin by being able to articulate *exactly* what you do.

Take a moment

Your goal here is to pull together an overview of your job. To identify what you are working on, where it is up to and so on. And to identify what you *will* be handing over, and what you *won't*.

This is no small task. As I'm sure your job is multifaceted and at times unpredictable.

Begin by gathering all the information you have available to you relating to your current role. This may include things such as:

- job description
- person specification
- your current objectives
- departmental objectives.

Check these for accuracy and update as necessary.

In addition to your formal documentation, which often describes what you do more or less accurately, there will be some things you do which aren't written down. The 'ad hoc' activities that come your way.

For example, a consultative role you play in a colleague's project, or an activity you've 'taken on' to fill in the gaps while no-one else was doing it.

So you need to capture this too.

I recommend you monitor this for a period of time, writing it down, and making sure it's in your handover folder.

This is you beginning to identify – with accuracy – what you *actually* do. Not just what people *think* you do.

Now some of this you will be expecting another person to do while you are on leave, and some you will not. It doesn't all automatically get handed over.

For example, depending on the length of your maternity leave, there may be projects that pause until you return, or there may be some that have to keep up momentum to reach a tight deadline.

So the next thing for us to do is to separate out what you are and are *not* handing over.

 Take a moment

Look back at the information you have gathered and highlight everything you *will* be handing over to someone while you're on leave.

Move these into the handover folder you are developing for your maternity cover.

Next, take the items you have **not** highlighted for handover and do the following.

- Identify things that will pause – make a note of who needs to know this is pausing.
- Identify things that will move to another person – make a note of who they are moving to.
- For anything that will be dropped – check you're sure this is OK. Consult others if you need to ensure they agree it's not going to be a problem.

So imagine that's Point A defined. The state of your 'work baby' right now, and how you are leaving it. We know where we are starting from.

But where are we heading? What about Point B? Let's turn our attention now to that. What 'state' you want things to be in when you return (see the next 'instalment' of 'Take a moment'.

 Take a moment

Visualize the month you plan to return in your mind. Whether it's six weeks, six months, or a year away. We know this can change but start with what you're planning for now.

Take the items you highlighted as being handed over to your cover.

Looking at each point individually, identify what you want it to look like when you return.

For example, you may be planning on taking six months off, and there's a project which needs to be at a specific point by that time.

Again write this down, capture it in the way that works best for you and add this detail to your handover folder.

You've worked out what state your work is in now, and what you want it to be like when you pick it up.

Before we move on, it's important to recognize, that even the best laid, well thought-through plans will experience disruption. That's life.

There are always things we can't control.

But there will be lots of things you can influence by way of a robust, thorough and well thought-through handover.

So let's look at step two.

Step two

Ask yourself: For a person to be able to do what's been listed in step one, what do they need to help them?

You know your role, some of you may know it intimately, able to work without thinking, or pausing to reflect. Some of you may be newer to your role, still thinking things through, finding the 'right people' to talk to, the 'latest document or protocol' for example.

I now want you to try to imagine you know *nothing*. You don't know who people are, where documents are kept, what systems to use, when meetings take place. You don't even know where to store your trainers or where to find the printer.

What you do know, because it's been outlined for you, is what the expectations are of you over the upcoming months.

To achieve those expectations, what do you need?

For this next exercise, I'd like you to put your 'new girl' hat on, and challenge everything, by imagining you know nothing about this particular role in this organization.

 Take a moment

What will your cover need to be successful in what you're asking them to do?

Here are some possible examples:

Context or background info – where it fits into bigger plans (dept/org strategy)

- System information, access
- Spreadsheets, data, progress reports

- Meeting schedules, purpose, and outcomes
- Contact details – specific people, helpful numbers, who's who?
- Training, coaching, skills support

These are prompts to get you thinking.

Now return to the points in your handover and take each one at a time, asking yourself what your cover will need.

Capture your responses, and once you've done this, be sure to update your handover file accordingly.

If you have an external candidate covering your role, your organization is likely to have an onboarding process which covers things like culture and other standard processes and expectations. These activities will all help your handover be effective too.

But your handover is still essential, and I hope when you look at how yours is developing you feel pleased and reassured.

It's a significant thing handing your role over, and for some of you it may feel particularly stressful, coming at a time where we know stress is something we want you to minimize… for *your* health, and for the health of your baby.

Step three

Ask yourself: How do I communicate this to increase the chances of success?

You've done a brilliant amount of thinking getting to this point. Hopefully this will serve you well when we move onto the next step.

How we communicate the things we are handing over.

Here's the next part of your 'Take a moment' activity for this chapter.

 Take a moment

Open your handover file, and for each thing you've identified ask yourself: 'Who needs to know this?'

For example, if you are handing over responsibility for organizing a particular monthly meeting, your cover, your line manager and meeting attendees may all need to know this.

Women usually find they begin to develop a list of things to communicate to their line manager, a list of things for their cover and so on.

Once you have done this, the next question is: *How?*

For example, you may need to communicate some things face to face, some via email, some in a written document and so on.

Again, through this process my clients usually find things begin to come together. For example, they may find that they need a 60-minute handover meeting with their line manager to tell them certain things, show them what's in different folders on the system, etc.

Identify how you want to communicate different things. Schedule when you are able to do this. Make it happen.

So that's it. Your handover.

The work that has meaning for you, properly thought through, therein creating the best possible chance of it being as you hope to find it when you return.

I hope that feels good, because it should. The peace of mind this can provide women with during their maternity leave is so important. I believe you deserve to focus on yourself and your baby on your leave and handing over well is a massive part in enabling this.

Before we close this chapter. There's one final step which is important for both you and your employer.

Final step

Ask yourself: To what extent do I want to be communicated with while I am off, and how?

I was talking to a line manager recently who was in a real pickle about one of her maternity leavers. She had been contacted by her direct report and asked for some information relating to her and her role, which she was really worried about responding to.

'What can I say, what can't I say. She's supposed to be on leave, I don't want to interrupt her time off with work things. It's not fair on her, it can wait… am I even *allowed* to communicate with her?!'

In my experience this dilemma and confusion between employer and employee is incredibly common. It can lead to uncomfortable situations, and on occasion to incredibly complicated and sometimes costly ones.

As with so many communication complexities they can often be avoided by upfront transparent dialogue, and subsequent agreements.

Which is the route we are going to take because it will be better for you, which matters. And better for your employer too.

Here's your exercise (see 'Take a moment').

Take a moment

Starting with your handover items.

What – if anything – do you want to know about these while you are away? Would you like to be updated on anything or nothing?

Reflect on your items and make a note of your thoughts.

Moving onto team and organization-related matters. What – if anything – would you like to be informed about? For example if you're a leader and member of your team leaves, would you like to know? Or if there's an office move that takes place and you move floor, would you like to know?

Reflect, and make a note of your thoughts.

As you work through this, pull together a list of situations, items that you *do* want to be told about. And things you do *not* want to have your maternity leave interrupted by.

The final piece here is to think about *how* you want this communication to take place. Email? A phone call? If you want to hear directly as opposed to on the fast (but often unreliable) grapevine, it's important you are clear.

As part of your handover to your line manager, add this to what you want to discuss in your face-to-face conversation.

Most line managers I've worked with are relieved at having this level of transparency.

Most women I've worked with are relieved at having this level of transparency.

I'd call that 'win-win'.

Depending on where you live, there will be legislation around what your organization can and *must* communicate to you. Restructures or redundancies are often examples of this. It's worth checking with your employer if you want to know more specifics.

I have clients who agree their 'keeping in touch' (KIT) days prior to their leave and how they will communicate about their focus for the day. I have clients who keep their KIT days as a flexible option to be agreed as it feels necessary.

I also have clients who formally agree the communication channel. For example, a female leader I worked with recently set up a new Gmail account specifically for her line manager to use to communicate with her about pre-agreed points. They agreed she would not access this account at all for the first eight weeks after her baby arrived. Then she would access it once a week on a Friday morning to see if there were any messages and, if so, she'd respond.

This would not be right for everyone, nor necessary. But this worked for her and for her employer.

My brilliant business partner 'redirected' my emails for a couple of weeks. He knows me well, and clearly knew that my self-discipline wouldn't be strong enough to resist checking in. So he wonderfully took the choice away from me. I was deeply appreciative.

I hope this process has enabled you to find *your* way. One that works for you, your employer and ultimately leaves you free to turn your attention to your baby safe in the knowledge that you've done everything you can to take care of your job too.

13
Planning your return to work

'I just want to be good at work and home'

Almost exactly four months after the arrival of her son, I spoke to one of my clients. She was *loving* motherhood. So much. However, she was worried. I asked her what about, and after twenty minutes of talking, it was evident that she was worried about a *lot*.

Still five months away, she was very worried about going back to work. She'd even started dreaming about it.

She was concerned about the specific timing of her return, and also about going back to a busy full-time role. She was concerned about the amount of travel involved – the time she would spend on trains and planes. She was concerned about navigating global calendars – the early mornings and late-night meetings needed, to cover other time zones.

Fundamentally, she was really concerned about being the mother who rarely saw her son, at most putting him to bed and then carrying on working.

To be fair, this kind of thing is worth being worried about.

I asked her what she wanted her return to be like. Which she found difficult to articulate.

Her connection with her own needs was vague. Drowned out in an ocean of expectations and assumptions.

There was a real and high risk of her agreeing to everything everyone else wanted and finding herself in a situation she hated. Not good for her, her home, baby or ultimately her employer. And she is a bright woman. She completely recognized this.

Preparing well for the return to work is such a significant point in the parental transition. It signifies the key intersection where working women who have become mothers become 'working mothers'.

No wonder it's challenging.

'Imagine there are no risks'

If I were to have a superpower, I know exactly which one I'd choose.

I'd like to be able to temporarily remove any risk and fear I feel in situations to enable me to think freely for a while.

With clients, *this* is what I try to tap into.

So, thinking about your return to work. Imagine if, just for now, there were no risks. Financial, security, emotional or of any other kind. What would you want your return to look like?

I asked my client this question, temporarily removing her worries. Her answers were suddenly crystal clear. 'I'd like to be self-led, to work with trusted autonomy. To have some flexibility, and not to go back full time straight away. Instead, I'd love an agreed and staged return.'

Now, *here* was something we could work with.

Let's see what this throws up for you. Here's something for you to do (see the following 'Take a moment'). You'll need a calm moment for this, free from interruptions.

 ### Take a moment

Take a piece of paper and pen. Please don't be worried about the blank nature of it — we're going to create something important here together.

Imagine there are **absolutely no risks**. Nothing to be worried about or scared of.

Answer this question:

What will your perfect work and home balance look and feel like?

It might be to be home for bath time, or to have a point mid-week where you work from home. It could be to have space to go to the gym, or the chance to reduce your travel time.

To begin with please don't overthink it. Try not to judge anything that comes to mind. Let your mind roam free.

Let go of any barriers that come to mind, we'll get to them soon enough.

Capture your thoughts.

How do you feel when you look at what you *really* want?

Some people can feel deeply connected and energized by the freedom of thinking about their needs and desires without limitations or restrictions. For others it can be a challenging, scary thing to do. Whatever *you* feel, just know that it's OK.

Now, there's a huge difference between acknowledging our feelings about what we want, and the choices we make about whether – or not – to act on them.

So having enjoyed the freedom of open thought, let's think about what we do with the things we've found.

Adding reality

I've offered you the opportunity to think freely just now. Removing restrictions, requirements and expectations. I've done this deliberately to try to tap into what your heart really wants.

In doing so, I have given you the opportunity to be truly honest with yourself, so you can see where you'd ideally like things to be.

The reality of life means that not all of this may be possible, but you never know.

Let's see what parts of your ideal we can keep and work towards. To do this we are going to bring the more practical, realistic lens *back* into our thinking.

This lens might feel quite familiar. It's the one that has an incredible knack of finding all manner of barriers. Such as, 'we can't afford it' or 'it's not possible to do my job in anything less than full time'.

And it's important we respect this lens. It's important we look at what is and isn't possible. It's important for you, your family and your security.

So let's get real in this next activity and build on your previous thinking.

 Take a moment

Let's move on and find all the **barriers** that will prevent your ideal from happening.

One by one, take the points you've captured in your ideal situation from the previous exercise, and write down all the reasons why you believe this is problematic. Or even impossible.

For example, I can't reduce my hours because we can't afford it, or I know my boss isn't open to flexible working because my colleague tried, and she was told 'no'.

Write it all down. Without judgement, and once you've done this, simply reflect on how you feel.

This process can be quite cathartic for some people. Clients often say that writing just out the barriers, fears and concerns helps with perspective, and frees them up from internal worrying. And once out, they can automatically begin to feel less scary or rigid.

By acknowledging them it's possible to see what exact hold they really have on your situation. You might be surprised that it's not as tricky as you think it is in some instances.

Some will be actual barriers, while others you might find aren't. For example, my client earlier thought her employer would say anything less than full time from the start was impossible. Interestingly, turns out that wasn't their view at all.

So it's also important we *challenge* this lens and separate out what is a 'real' barrier and what isn't, as it's highly likely that many of your barriers are fuelled by a whole heap of **assumptions**.

Assumptions

Assumption: A thing that is accepted as true or as certain to happen, without proof

Why would we accept something is certain to happen if we don't have proof to confirm this is the case?

Would you accept that your investment of £1,000 is going to grow to £10,000 if you hadn't had some sort of evidence this was true?

Would you take a chance on living in a new area just because you read about it without either knowing people who live there, visiting it or finding out for yourself?

Probably unlikely. It's more likely that you'd assume a visit to the area would give you useful, additional insight.

We *all* hold assumptions – and some of them are helpful and some of them aren't.

For example if I assume someone might resist some feedback I have to offer, it could be helpful in ensuring I'm careful and clear about what I am saying. Or it could be unhelpful as it could prevent me from sharing the feedback at all for fear of the response.

So, it's useful to challenge our assumptions, because some of them will be true and helpful, but some might not, and instead are simply holding you back.

In coaching work, we often address assumptions: 'You think that, but what evidence do you have to say that it's true?'

The process underpinning this follows the broad structure listed here.

1. Let's identify your ideal scenario – think freely for a moment.
2. Let's get practical and think of all the barriers that stand in the way to achieving this ideal.
3. Let's challenge these barriers to see if they are real or not. Are they based on evidence, on fact – or on assumption you are holding?

Together, thinking about your return to work, we've already done points 1 and 2. So let's now extend our thinking through the activity that follows.

 Take a moment

Draw a line down the centre of a blank page. On one side write 'Fact' and on the other side 'Assumption'.

Next, take your barriers one at a time, and ask yourself:

Is this barrier based on evidence, on fact – or on assumption you are holding?

If it is a fact. Write it in the 'fact' column.

If it is an assumption. Write it in the 'assumption' column.

Really challenge yourself to be super clear and *only* put evidenced facts in the fact column.

For example, if you have heard from a colleague's experience that asking for condensed hours will be rejected, this counts as an assumption. You are assuming that your experience will be the same.

If, however, you've asked your boss if you can agree condensed hours and they have said absolutely not and given you evidence of why, then this is a fact. You are clear about the situation. Whether you like this or not is separate as is how you respond. But it's fact. For now.

Once you've done this for all your barriers. Pull your insight together. What does this tell you?

For example, you might have realized you are assuming that your finances are limiting you but have realized that you don't know this for sure. As it's a while since you've looked really closely at your household budgets and things have changed.

Or you might be assuming that a full-time nursery place won't be available at your local childcare provider, because a friend told you her child had been on the waiting list since they were three months old, but you haven't visited and asked them directly.

As always, don't judge yourself. Just pull your refined thoughts together. You'll end up with your barriers separated out into those we know to be true, and those we don't. Yet.

Once you've done this, how do you feel?

Assumptions are perfectly natural for our human brains. We typically use them to help us navigate our circumstances and to control the outcomes. For example, I might assume it's not safe to walk through a park because no-one else seems to be doing it. Therefore I don't in the hope I get home safely.

Or I might assume the best thing to do is to give my child soft food when weaning them because that's what I see and hear other people doing. I do this in the hope I've given my child the most nutritional start to life.

But if assumptions are 'thing(s) accepted as true... without proof' then couldn't it be considered tantamount to guessing? And I doubt any of us agree that playing 'guess your future' at this stage in your life is good way to go.

No. We want to take control, understand what we are dealing with and use this to make our own **choices**. Free will, and freedom of choice is one of our core human rights. So let's be sure to exercise it.

Exercising choice

Choice: An act of deciding between two or more possibilities

My client held an assumption that because she'd said she thought she'd go back full time to her business, that this was what she had to do. There would be uncomfortable consequences otherwise.

She had no proof for this. Why? Because she hadn't yet mentioned this as a possibility to her employer. She assumed they'd say 'no' but she didn't know for sure.

This was sitting in her 'assumptions' not 'fact' column.

I asked her how we turn this assumption into a fact? She responded clearly and said: 'I need to talk to my boss.'

I asked her all the ways in which her boss could respond. In theory. And there were several potential responses on the cards.

- Absolutely not. It's full time or nothing.
- We can do a staged return over a few weeks but not over a six-week period.
- Yes, we can look into making that work.

We'd prepared her for all of these possibilities, by working through 'If they say X, where does that leave you?', providing her with thought through responses along the way. These included: 'Thanks; let me take that information away and think about it', to 'I love my work, and I really want to find a way that works for all of us, so what are our next steps to working this out'.

Once prepared, she found the courage and talked to her boss. She asked her if she'd consider a six-week staged return to work, starting with part time and building up to full hours.

What are the actions you could take to turn your assumptions into facts? Let's move towards tangible actions in the final part of this activity.

 Take a moment

Go back to the points in your assumption column.

Now, ask yourself these questions.

- What proof do I need to find out whether this assumption is real or not?
- How do I get that proof?

Use this to develop a series of actions for yourself – such as these two examples.

- Review the household finances.
- Plan, arrange and have a conversation with your boss.

Don't over complicate things. The actions may seem very simple, but if they provide you with your answers that's all we are looking for.

As you look at your list of actions, prioritize them. Identify which can be done swiftly, easily and by you. Which need to be done first. Which are going to take time and involve other people? Which you need to prepare for?

Then it's a matter of taking your list, and making the actions happen starting at the top and moving on down.

So here it is. That's what you need to do.

Once you have proof then the guesswork can stop. Now you're dealing in facts, facing reality.

Now you can make your choices. What do the facts tell you?

They may tell you that you need to stay where you are for a while. They may tell you that you have more options than you think. They may tell you that it's time to start looking for new employment. They may tell you so many things.

You may like what they tell you. Or you might not.

But at least you're in control. At least you are clear, and you can make choices. This is empowering. Now you know for sure what is and isn't possible.

I know when I was on maternity leave with my first son, I held a massive assumption about needing to go back to work early. Being self-employed, any benefits to cover my salary were very limited. My partner and I really challenged this assumption by working out all our finances. So many numbers! Looking at what we thought we spent versus what we did indeed spend, where we could cut budgets and so on.

Not a process I enjoyed at all I must say, but one that needed to be done to allow us to make an informed decision.

I talked to my business partner about options, and eventually when all of this came together it turned out I was working on a pretty accurate assumption. I *did* need to go back to work quickly but... I didn't need to go back full time for quite a while.

This helped massively and enabled me to go from feeling 'not at all OK' about it to 'OK'. I felt as if I was in control, I was exercising all the choices that were available to me. And with this control came a level of acceptance and empowerment. Which changed everything.

I believe we can make things work for us. Maybe not in one go, but incrementally, slowly nudging towards our ideal. We need to be supported, clear, flexible and courageous. But with effort and thought, amazing outcomes can be found.

My client asked her boss and negotiated a three-month staged return. It worked for everyone. She was clear, content and felt valued. She was better at work, and at home as a result.

I'd call this a success story.

I wish you every success in nudging closer and closer to that ideal *you* envisage.

14
Navigating your first few months back

'I'm so sorry, I've got to go'

My friend Claire woke up one morning in a different world. Same bed. Same partner. Same baby.

But Claire wasn't the same.

Claire would not be the Claire she was yesterday *ever* again.

No. Claire was off to work.

Let's talk about your return to work, now that you're a parent.

Crack on!

On the bookshelves of many new CEOs you'll find one about the significance of their first 90 days in post. The book strapline says it all:

'Proven strategies for getting up to speed faster *and* smarter' (Watkins, 2003).

A whole book on fast approaches to integrating yourself into a workplace with impact in your first 90 days in the role.

Ninety days = three months.

And *this* is the 'pacey' approach.

Now I think this is a great book, and it's helped lots of clients I've worked with over the years in planning their arrival into a new role. Enabling them to bring people with them and maximize their positive impact.

But... here's my pause for thought.

What do you reckon the grace period offered to women returning from maternity leave is?

How long do you think they are given before being expected to be 'back up to speed'?

Ninety days? Three months?

No chance.

Aah, but they aren't new are they? They are *returning*.

They know the job, they know the business, they know the strategy, they know the people. Of course they do.

Because nothing ever changes. Time, people, and businesses stand still.

Time travel

What about you? Have you been standing still over the last few weeks or months?

Why don't we see?

I'm going to take us back in time and for ease, let's go back 12 months. A year.

This time last year...

This time last year, my oldest son hadn't started playing ball hockey. Now he's squad number 42 (the meaning of life) and fully immersed in his club.

This time last year, my younger son hadn't yet met the teacher who was going to inspire him like no other. He hadn't read *Moby Dick*, learned about the Romans, or realized that with incredibly hard work he could play 'Ode to Joy' on his violin.

This time last year, I hadn't started writing a book. This book. I hadn't realized that I could create more space in my life, juggle more balls and make it work.

This time last year, British politics was messy, and over the last year we've learned it can get even messier.

This time last year, I hadn't realized that my next car would be green, and my partner and I hadn't realized that we'd suddenly lose one of his close friends to cancer.

I wonder what's happened in your life recently?

Here's an activity to help you reflect on this.

 Take a moment

Take a piece of paper and write down today's date along with the date when you left your workplace to go on leave. This might be 6 weeks ago, 4 months or maybe 12+ months ago.

Thinking back over that period, begin to capture what has changed for you. Think about events, about things you've learned about people and the environment around you.

Once you've done this take a moment to reflect on what you've written and the impact these changes have had on you.

When I reflect, I realize that the events of the last 12 months in my life have brought my attention back to my own immediate family. To our needs at this point in our lives.

The last 12 months have shifted where I put my focus, time and energy. What I worry about and what I don't. For example, I no longer resist being the 'taxi' service all weekend as a big part of my purpose right now is to facilitate the lives of my children, and to help them learn to socialize in the world around them.

Below are a few prompts to help deepen your reflections. Feel free to add your own questions in too.

- What are you better at now than you were before maternity leave?
- What are you clearer about now than you were before maternity leave?
- What do you know that you didn't before maternity leave? About yourself, others, the world
- What are you completely certain about now, that you only had an inkling about before maternity leave?
- What's the same as it was before maternity leave? What has remained for you?

And then…

How might all of this inform the needs of the woman who is going back to work?

When you step back into your workplace, who is that woman who is walking through the door? She may look very similar, but I wonder what's going on inside her.

What is the same and what has changed? What does she *need?*

Write down your **needs**. These may be practical – i.e. time-related. They may be emotional – i.e. support-related. They may be something entirely different. Either way you need them, and therefore they matter.

Pause and reflect on how you feel having worked through this process.

When we cast our minds back in time and reflect, one thing will be evident for certain.

Nothing will be exactly the same. Everything will have changed to some extent.

So, the woman who 'left' work to have a baby is not going to be the same and the one who 'returns'. She may be stronger; she may feel weaker. She may have a different focus, she may have a new interest. She may be more content, or she may not.

Either way, she's informed by her new experiences. And that's important for both her, and her employer, to know.

And she's not the only thing to have changed. There's certainly going to have been a lot of change in her workplace too.

Returner or new starter?

As a business coach I have a kind of triangular pattern in most of my relationships. There's me – there's the coachee – and then there's the employer. The business that has commissioned my work.

As part of this dynamic, it's common (within agreed boundaries) for me to advise the employer of the person I'm working with, on ways in which they can support them internally.

The very first thing I say to employers when talking about a woman coming back from maternity leave is: 'Please do not think of her as a returner. Nothing is the same. You have a different woman coming back to a different business. The very best thing you can do for this woman is support and onboard her the way you would a **new starter**. Because *she* needs to get to know you, and *you* need to get to know her.'

New starters in many organizations get treated to a grace period when they first arrive. Granted, not everywhere, and this time definitely varies from place to place. But for most of us, there's a 'landing zone' where we are typically given time to get our heads around our new job.

Whether through informal or formal induction processes we are usually given information to help us with this. Information about things such as:

- the business strategy, culture and vision
- core business objectives, products and areas of focus
- 'who's who' – introductions to the people in the business, our line manager and colleagues
- team information in the form of who does what – roles, responsibilities and remits
- our goals and objectives outlining what we are there to do and how we will be measured
- practical information about where to find information, systems to access and processes to follow
- practical information about meetings, weekly diary structures and significant business events.

Sometimes induction processes are planned over a day, sometimes over a period of weeks. Some take place face to face, others in written form.

Alongside this, it's widely recognized that we need to allow the new starter time to develop relationships with people. Sometimes 'coffee introductions' are set up to encourage this process, or people are invited to 'away days' before they start, to encourage interaction.

Human Resource teams often put effort into this 'onboarding' process: the view that if people are brought into the organization more effectively, they are likely to embed themselves more smoothly. Leading to a happier and more impactful employee and in turn a more content employer too.

It strikes me as obvious a new parent returning from parental leave might benefit from this level of care to a greater or lesser extent too. Don't you think?

Sadly, in my experience, few women returning from maternity leave are offered the same level of support as a new starter. Some are, but they remain a minority.

I asked my friend Claire about her return. Her response was that her desk had been moved, so she didn't know where to sit to begin with, and her line manager wasn't in. No one had expected her to arrive, as her maternity cover hadn't worked out so had left a few weeks beforehand. Her inbox was full, and there was a meeting in her diary for 2pm with a new direct report.

Great first day, which left her feeling really disorientated. And lots of other things on the side.

What I see from my clients is an experience more akin to a baton being handed over in a relay race. 'Thanks goodness you're back; now let's keep going.' And so the woman gets caught in the whirlwind of her two worlds, sometimes hanging on for dear life.

To be fair, I have some incredible clients who plan and support new returning parents amazingly.

One lady recently told me that she'd even received an email from their global CEO welcoming her back and reassuring her that she'd already proved herself to them, so just to continue being herself now she was back as a working mother. She wasn't even his direct report, yet his email made such a difference to her. This kind of story makes my heart sing!

It's not the norm though. Not yet. Maybe together we can try to change it for the future workplaces our children will inhabit if they become working parents? I fundamentally believe we should be setting ourselves – and others – up for success as opposed to failure.

And we can start, by taking control of the situation ourselves.

It's important to recognize *what* we need, and if it's not on offer, to ask for it.

When working with clients, I ask questions such as these.

- What do you need to know about the business?
- What would you like to know about any strategic or structural changes?
- What would you like to know about any people changes that have taken place?
- What information will it be helpful for your line manager to share with you?
- What work will you be doing and how will you be measured on it?
- What projects were you working on before you left that you'd like to hear an update on?

Writing this, I'm thinking of a lady I coached a few years ago, who worked her way through this process in the months before she was due to return to work. She took the time to really think about what she needed and work out a plan to satisfy these needs.

She contacted her HR rep and asked for some of these things to be sent to her as she needed them in advance.

Other things she wanted to get through informal routes. So she met up with a few colleagues for coffee and drinks and found out the 'insider news'.

She used a couple of her remaining 'Keep in Touch' (KIT) days to meet with her line manager, and other internal colleagues to be updated on specific things that would help her when she returned. She talked to her line manager about how she wanted to run the first few weeks of her diary – new people she wanted to be introduced to, meetings she wanted to begin by 'sitting in on' and so on.

She also used part of a KIT day to hang out with her maternity cover, to find out more about her work, and what she was coming back to.

I can tell you that without doubt, this level of planning and preparation served her well. She was happier and more in control when the day came for her to formally 'return'.

Now, the approach this client took may not be the right one for you. We have different jobs, different levels of autonomy, different needs. However, the principle she followed *will* be right.

The more in control you feel, the more confident and effective you will be.

Contributing to change

The range of experiences women have returning to work from any length of maternity leave is so varied. From Claire's experience where no one was there or ready for her, to a woman receiving a 'we've got you' message from a CEO.

I believe so strongly that if we want women to thrive when they return, this particular moment is a critical one. And one that requires attention and improvement. And as with most things in life if it's not forthcoming, we have to go and get it.

Claire and I talked. And she decided she wanted to tell her employer how she'd felt. They asked her if she'd help them to learn from her experiences, and with her own generosity and kindness, she helped them to understand her experience. And together they'd changed things for the returning parents in their organization for the better.

I'm proud of Claire, and of the positive change she made happen. Not only for herself, but for other working mothers in her business in the future.

Maybe you're part of changing things for your future colleagues too?

Part six
Strategies for planning your future

15
Your future

I've always wanted to...'

I phoned a family member one day, and during a bit of chit chat, they asked me: 'What have you got planned for the weekend?'

What? My mind went blank. I wasn't sure what day it even was, let alone what I was up to on the weekend... And don't get me started on the date, month, or year. I'm stuck in the tail end of the 1990s somewhere.

You'll agree, I suspect, that our ability to think in the short and long term changes as we move through the working parenthood transition.

When we are in the thick of life with a new baby, getting our heads around the next half hour can sometimes feel a stretch. When we first return to work, getting out of the door can feel akin to climbing Everest.

But slowly, gradually, almost unnoticeably, this changes. Once again, the waves of psychological transition work their magic on our thinking.

There comes a point, where we no longer feel like we are chasing out tails quite as much as we have been doing. At least not *all the time* anyway. At this point our thoughts start casting themselves wider and further afield. Maybe wondering whether we might take a break this summer, musing about what life might have in store for us over the next few years, or thinking about what we want from our work. Now that a child is here.

You may already be finding that time feels like it has more future to it again. And if you don't – no need for concern, be assured this will eventually come. Trust the process. Trust that your body and your brain know what to do. They've spent a long time evolving.

We've talked in previous chapters about your short-term needs, but now it's time for us to shift our attention to the longer term. To begin to think bigger and further ahead.

It's time to go on a different type of journey.

North-east or south-west?

My client simply stood up and walked out of a meeting and out of work one day. She got in her car and urgently drove home.

As an area manager for a retail brand, she spent a lot of her time away. Every week, for several nights at a time, across her large geographical region, supporting her teams. Her children had been in nursery when she took this role, and now they were getting ready for secondary school. She couldn't believe how quickly the time had gone.

At home the previous weekend, she'd felt oddly out of sync with the rest of her family. She described how she'd felt more like a visitor in her own home than she felt comfortable with.

In that meeting she had realized that she'd been working away for a lot longer than she'd *ever* anticipated. And with that, she had missed a lot of important family life. Everyday time, simple experiences that she wasn't going to be able to get again.

Hurtling up the motorway, she was urgently heading home to fix something she'd only just realized needed fixing.

She was driving to fix her life.

As I'm writing this, I'm struck by how many stories I could have shared with you in this particular chapter. They are plentiful. Experience after experience shared in coaching about how small, micro choices can turn out once they're all pieced together.

Because life isn't one big thing. It's not massive leaps, but a series of smaller things all put together to create one journey.

And like all other journeys, we start at the start, and we will end at the end. We may stop at a few service stations along the way, be sent on a couple of unexpected diversions and there's no doubt that we will sit in traffic for a while. Some of the roads will be fully lit, and others will seem dark. Some will straight and open, others narrow and bendy.

And usually, we're OK with that as long as the end point is where we wanted to go in the first place.

But what happens when we don't know our destination? What happens when we just end up 'somewhere' and we're not entirely sure we like it?

My client didn't know her destination. By her own admission, she'd been taking her journey 'leg by leg' and making decisions in isolation along the way.

She'd been speeding along, heading South.

But what if I told you that it turned out her desired destination was actually North?

The 'micro decisions' she'd made along the way, weren't necessarily wrong. They were made with the information she had to hand at the time. But... they were made in *isolation*, without a handle on the bigger picture they needed to feed into.

Realizing this had shocked her. But it had also focused her and enabled her to change her course of travel before it was too late. Through hard work, and time, through new decisions set within a bigger context, she moved her life back to travelling in the right direction for her.

She had a happy ending. Which pleases me greatly, as she really deserved it.

Shall we look at your direction of travel, and see if you're heading towards your desired destination? It may seem daunting, but trust me you'll benefit, and I wonder if you might even find it fun.

Visioning your future

Visioning: The process of imagining how things will develop in the future and planning how to make it happen

So far in this book, we've done a lot of work on connecting you with who you are right now, looking at what matters to you, what you've learned from your journey into working parenthood, and what energizes you. Grounding you in the present.

Now let's think differently.

I'm going to go in big, and see how you feel about a question a bit like this...

What do you want your life to be like ten years from now?

Hmmm that's a new type of challenge isn't it! You might be thinking 'not got a clue, can barely think about next week', maybe you're feeling excited by finding an answer to this or alternatively quite daunted. You may already know, in which case use this chapter to confirm what you believe to be true.

What I can guarantee is that many of you will have cast your minds forward to how old this will make you. Then your thoughts will have quickly been followed by 'oh my days, that's not too far away... !'

So, how old will you be? How old will your partner be, your child or children, your wider family, your friends? Get them in mind because they will play a significant part in this.

We are going to build up a picture of how you want your life to *feel*. What do you want to focus on, how do you want to use this thing called 'time'?

I want us to work deeply on this, so below is something to do. This exercise is one to start, leave to settle, pick up again, so you don't need a big block of time in one go. It's an activity to enjoy getting curious about. Patiently over moments that lie ahead, you're going to build up a picture for you to work towards making happen.

 ## Take a moment

I'd like you to take your time to answer the set of questions that follow. Be patient with yourself, as some answers will come easily and some may feel harder to find.

If you get stuck on a question, move on to the next one, and come back to it when you're ready.

What's important is not to think about the 'how'. Don't worry about how likely this is to happen, or how to make any of it happen. We will get to that. Just let your hopes and dreams flow.

Pen and paper ready? Here are your questions.

Cast your mind forward ten years, thinking about the 'X-year-old you'.

- How do you want her life to be?
- How is she living? Describe it – maybe how it feels, looks or sounds
- How is she spending her time? What is she focusing on?
- What matters to her? What is important in her life?
- Who is around her? What people and things does she surround herself with?
- What is her environment like? What kind of space is she living in? What is she seeing each day?
- What hobbies or interests will she be engaging in?
- What kind of money will she have or need?
- What role will travel play in her life?
- What kind of work will she be doing? How will she be working?
- How important is learning to her? What might she have learned or still be learning?
- How important is autonomy to her? To what extent will she be 'self-led'?
- How important is impact to her? How might she be making a difference to the people and things around her?
- What will she be known for – by her family, friends, colleagues and community?
- How old will her child(ren) be, and what needs will they have of her?
- Who will she be living with and what are their needs likely to be? What are their hopes and aspirations for this period?

Gradually, as you work through these questions, begin to build up a picture of the life you wish for yourself in ten years' time.

As your thoughts settle, bring them together in one place. Some people choose to write, some to draw. One woman I worked with drew a picture of the life she was working towards. It involved a clear image of the home she'd be living in. Completely out of the blue, eight years after drawing the image, she sent me a picture of her new home. It even had the flowers in the garden she'd dreamed of.

Once you have done this, reflect on what it tells you. See if you can draw out your key themes. The points that *really matter* to you in all of this.

For example, there may be a strong pull to move to the country from the city, or to live overseas. There may be a strong pull to have more control over your time, more flexibility in the way you operate. Of there may be a driving goal to have financial freedom.

How do you feel when you reflect on what you'd like to achieve in the next ten years? Don't judge it, but simply notice for now.

People can find that when they create a vision of their future self, it confirms some of what they know already. Things that they may already be working towards, like living in a certain part of the country or developing a new area of knowledge.

Others can find surprises crop up. Things they had dismissed as less important, or unattainable. For example, requalifying and starting a new career or becoming self-employed.

In my experience, everyone has aspects of their future vision they feel they can execute and make happen, alongside other areas that are going to require more thought and planning – to see if they are even possible.

In a moment, I'm going to offer you the opportunity to build on what you've worked out so far and start thinking about 'how' to turn this vision into a reality.

Your brain will do a brilliant job at trying to protect you from 'perceived risks' as you go through this process. Finding all manner of ways to tell you it's not possible.

Remember, we are just *thinking* at this stage. Just working it through, so try to keep your mind open to possibilities for now. The 'reality' will kick in soon enough, and then we will work it through in a sensible way.

So, if you completed the earlier activity questions, and have a 'vision' of the future you'd like for yourself in ten years' time, here is the next piece of thinking for you to do.

Again, this may take time. We're in no immediate rush, so allow your thoughts to take the time they need.

 Take a moment

Take your vision as you understand it so far. Then work through the following questions, capturing your responses as you go along.

- What are your top priorities? The things you feel strongly about making happen. Draw out the most pressing or important ones for you.

These are likely to be ones you have a strong 'feeling' towards. This is important. Acknowledge that feeling. Your body is working hard to tell you something, even if your brain can't quite articulate it yet.

- Who do you need to involve as you explore these priorities?

Your partner, for example, to see if this aligns with their needs, or an expert such as a financial adviser or someone at your bank.

- What are the most obvious actions that need to happen for you to be clearer about how to make these are reality?

For example, if retraining is on your list, you might need to find out places and costs associated with doing so. Then sit down with your finances, and get planning if/how/when you can build this in.

Consider what – if any – order these things need to happen in. For example, if you want to move house, but to do so you need to increase your income, or get a handle on your saving needs, then focusing on this must come first.

Finally, see if there are any timeframes for these actions. They may be loose or – pending what you have in mind – they may be set in stone. For example, if one of your plans is fixed around a child moving to senior school you will know the year this will be. Other things might be – for example – to retrain over the next two or three years.

You should begin to see a plan emerging. A plan of small things that sit within some level of your control. As you know from previous chapters we've worked through together – start with the things you can do something about. This is the way we take control and move forward.

I was working with a client recently, who conducted the activity you've just completed.

I asked her how she felt when she'd done it. 'Excited!' she said.

What does yours look like I wonder, and how does it make you feel? Mine often makes me feel 'relieved'. Why? Because I like a plan, a shared plan with my partner. And I believe once things are transparent between us we can work together towards turning things into a reality.

I hope it also tells you about the significance of the choices you make *today*. Because every step counts.

Know *your* 'North Star'

Through the words on the pages of this book, we have worked together through some core principles aimed at grounding you to your sense of 'self'.

We've looked at your values, your strengths and your motivators.

We've connected you to your short-term goals, and not your long-term aspirations. Giving you not just a sense of who you are today, but a sense of who you aim to become. The life you will work to have for yourself.

Like having a clear destination on a journey.

But like every journey, there will be twists and turns. We know things don't always go exactly to plan. So we've also worked through strategies to help you when things get tough. Techniques to help you manage your fear, maximize your learning and regain control.

We've found insights for you to anchor yourself with when it comes to making decisions, choices and managing setbacks along the way.

My client gave herself an 18-month timeframe to change her work so she could be based at home.

But she started talking to her family that very day once she'd driven up the motorway.

And she started planning the change with her partner in the following weeks, talking to her employer about her concerns roughly a month after she'd walked out of the meeting.

In the end, it took her just 14 of the 18 months.

And *everyone* was happy.

16
Your support network

'Can someone help me?'

By now you know that the journey you are on is seismic. And you also know that the journey you are on is rewarding, albeit challenging.

What this journey *doesn't* have to be is lonely...

Who's supporting you?

I recall, more than 15 years ago, one of my mentors saying to me: 'Look behind you – who's on your bench?'

I tentatively looked around, confused and wondering what on earth he was talking about.

Turns out he was talking about something really significant and very powerful, which I actively still think about myself, and work on with my coaching clients too.

My mentor was talking about my 'supporters'. He was talking about the people I turn to when I need help, answers, insight and care. The people who I know I can trust to 'have my back' and to keep me on track. People who are there for a reason and purpose, and ready to be called upon when the time comes.

I wonder what names and faces are coming into your mind as you think about this.

Maybe your colleagues past or present. Maybe friends or loved ones. Maybe professionals – some of whom you pay to support you – like therapists, mentors and coaches.

You may find you reach out to these people for slightly different things. One may be a shoulder to cry on, another a person to celebrate your 'wins' with.

The distinction here is important, as really effective support networks have different people for different reasons.

Supporting roles

Support: To help someone emotionally or in a practical way

Support comes in lots of different forms. By definition, sometimes it's emotional and sometimes it's practical. Often we offer support because we want someone to succeed.

I want all women to succeed in motherhood. I want all working women to succeed in their role. And I want all working mothers – just like me and you – to succeed in both.

The support I offer to achieve this is both emotional and practical, but it's also formal, because I as a professional am engaged specifically to do this.

Let me add some structure to this for you.

We know that there are six important roles we need to have filled, in a healthy support network. In no particular order, here they are.

1. The emotional supporter

This is the person who provides you with emotional support when you need it.

This could be in the form of a partner or friend you seek counsel from over a chat on the sofa, or someone more formal like a counsellor or therapist.

2. The motivator

This is the person who encourages you, who is 'on your side' and who recognizes everything you have worked to achieve. The big and small wins are all noted and brought to your attention.

This could be a line manager who notes how impressed they are by your handover, or a partner who says: 'Look at what you've managed to achieve this week!'

3. The collaborator

This is someone who is in the same situation as you – facing similar challenges and dilemmas.

My biggest collaborators in my own first maternity transition were my antenatal class 'girls'. We spent hours talking (and crying) together about ways to overcome reflux, manage sleep patterns and weaning. Sometimes over a walk in a park, sometimes over cake and coffee.

4. The linker

This is someone who connects you with other people who will help you. People with good networks, who trust you and are willing to generously share their contacts with you.

This might be a work colleague, or someone who runs a group of like-minded people for example. Or the friendly new parent in the park who asks you to come and join something they are heading off to do.

5. The mentor

This is a person who has trodden the path you are treading some time before. Mentors are often a good few steps ahead in their journey and have learned a lot along the way. The key thing about the mentor is that they are willing and able to share their wisdom with you.

It's common in the parenthood transition for people to have mentors from within their friends and family networks. Some people have their own mother in this role, or maybe siblings. Others seek this from friends who are further down the motherhood line. Professional colleagues who are already doing 'the juggle' can frequently fulfil this role too.

6. The coach

This role is there to help people navigate specific areas of challenge or concern. As you know it's the role I mainly sit in.

This role can be filled by professionals like me, or through books like this one.

Democratizing the maternity coaching process was one of my key drivers when writing this book for you. So everyone could experience and benefit from maternity coaching. Not just those lucky enough to access it through their employer.

And remember, I mentioned earlier that if you want to understand more about coaching – what it is and how it works – there are some recommendations for you in the 'Further reading' section at the back of this book.

So six roles. With different purposes but all focused on supporting *you*.

People in your support network might fill more than one of these roles; an emotional supporter is often a motivator, a collaborator might also be someone who is able to connect you to others.

Also, you may have several people fulfilling one role. I have three mentors for example. They are all brilliant and share wisdom on slightly different things.

Here is an activity to help you think about, and further develop, your own support network.

 Take a moment

Find something to write on and write down the roles I've just talked through. Leave a gap between them, so you have space to write.

Then go back to the top of your list. For each role, reflect on who you already have in place, and add names of people you could – or would like to – have in that role.

Think about personal contacts, work contacts, people you speak to regularly, people you've not spoken to for a while. It doesn't matter. We are just gathering potential names at this stage.

Some you will have lots of names against, some just one or two, and you may find you've a couple of roles with no-one against them at all. That's OK.

What do you notice when you look at this list? Are you pleased with what you see? Or concerned about the bits that are missing? Don't judge yourself, just notice.

We will work more on this in a moment.

In reality most of us have support networks that are populated 'to some extent', and we rely on a small number of people to fulfil a majority of roles. Where this is fine, and certainly better than having no one in place, it can be fragile.

Ideally, we want a robust network which draws on a range of people all ready and prepared to support in the *way* we need and *when* we need it.

Building your network of support

Clients typically realize they are missing support at the exact moment they need it most.

Imagine you look around to see who is ready to step up and support you and… no one is there.

I remember a coaching client a few years ago who was in the last few weeks before her maternity leave. Sadly, she was in a terrible place.

As a manager she was in a business she no longer felt part of and with a team that was struggling. She had a terrible relationship with her own line manager and felt very isolated.

At home she was away from her family, with a partner who was away working a lot of the time.

I think it's fair to say she felt very alone.

I'm pained to say this – but she was. And she was seeing this at the time she needed help most.

So how do we prevent this?

Ideally, we populate and care for our networks on an ongoing basis. I think of mine as being like a beautiful garden. One that needs to be prepared before seedlings can be planted. One that must be fed and watered regularly, then nurtured to enable the flowers to grow.

There's no time too soon with regards to doing this, and if you completed the earlier exercise, you've already begun making good progress.

The next step is to get in contact with those people – to reach out, meet and talk about your situation. To sound them out about whether they are happy to have a role and support your transition from being a working woman, to a working mother.

 Take a moment

Look back at your list. Highlight the key people you want, need and *can* focus on. This may be a long list, or a short one. What's important is that it's intentional and manageable for you at this moment in time.

Look at the names and draw out the people who already know they play this role for you. For example, your close friend may be well aware that they provide you with emotional support.

For these names ask yourself whether there's any benefit to recognize that with them, to note it with them and further cement it. There might or might not be.

Now turn your attention to the other names you highlighted. Ask yourself the following questions.

- How am I going to reach out to this person?
- What am I going to say and ask of them when I do?
- Does this relationship need 'formalizing'? For example is payment being made.
- How might I be able to help them in return? Maybe there's something reciprocal here.

In answering these questions you will be identifying actions to take and drawing up a list.

> Then, as you've already learned, prioritize those actions, and start making them happen.
>
> One at a time.

In my view – we would *all* benefit from developing, growing and caring for our support network on an ongoing basis. No matter what our role or stage in life. Parents, leaders, colleagues, young people and so on.

I encourage you to share as many aspects of this book with the people you share your parenting with as you think useful – but *especially* the content of this chapter. We all need to be supported fully during times of significant change.

Just remember, the importance of **nurturing** these relationships so when the time comes when we need advice, an ear, or a voice to help us, we simply turn around and there are people ready and willing to help.

The rule of reciprocity

Reciprocity is about exchange. In the field of social psychology there's robust work evidencing that if something good happens to us, we are more likely to do something good in response. If we experience kindness, we are more likely to respond with kindness. Phrases such as 'what goes around comes around' and 'do good, get good' are well-known examples of this principle.

One evidenced 'universal trust' in relation to human persuasion is considered to be that of **reciprocity** (Cialdini, 2007). There's evidence that humans not only like, but might even feel 'obliged', to return a favour if offered one by another first.

When we apply this idea to our support network principle it throws up lots of mutually beneficial opportunities. We support someone and they either support us – or another – in return. We pass on our wisdom gained, and another shares theirs with us.

There's something so comforting about this principle in the world of maternity coaching.

If we think back to traditions, it's common for generations of women to pass on their learning to each other whether through families or friendship circles. We all know it takes a 'village' to pull together to bring up a child. .

This prompts a very important question.

Whose support network are *you* in? And whose *could* you be in?

Maybe there's someone out there in need of support who you could reach out to today.

You are *not* alone

Although the journey you are on will change your life, it resembles one that has been trodden by many people before, and it will undoubtedly be trodden by people again.

Take comfort in this, by nurturing and utilizing your full support network, and sharing what you have learned for the benefit of others.

That's the way it has always been and will continue to be even as the generations come and go through the passage of time.

Conclusion

'You've got this'

So we are at the end of our time together. The chapters are complete, which leaves me one final chance to tell you what I really think of you.

I think you are impressive.

I have so much respect for you, and for *all* working mothers.

Not because we are perfect. On the contrary, because we are scarred.

Not because we've nailed it. No, but because we navigate a conveyor belt of conundrums, dilemmas and challenges on a daily basis.

And somehow, we find a way to keep going. Limping at times, dancing exquisitely at others.

I'm impressed because of the *effort* you put in, the constant evolution of who you are, and who you will continue to become. Because of the resilience you show. Day after day. Year after year.

I hope this book has shown you that you *have* choices. We always have choices. And I hope the strategies we've explored together empower you to make choices that work not only for your family, your employer but for *you* too.

I want our children to live in a world where we accept people can be brilliant at work and also at home. I want our children to know that people like us worked hard to create change and to be part of making this possible for them.

So close your eyes, take a deep breath and use the tools I've shared to support, empower and lead you to action.

Hold the hands of your loved ones. Squeeze them tightly, connect deeply, and off you go.

You've got this.

Appendices

Appendix A: Parental Transition Model, © Motion Learning, 2023

Appendix B: Possible Human Values, © Motion Learning, 2023

Appendix A: Parental Transition Model

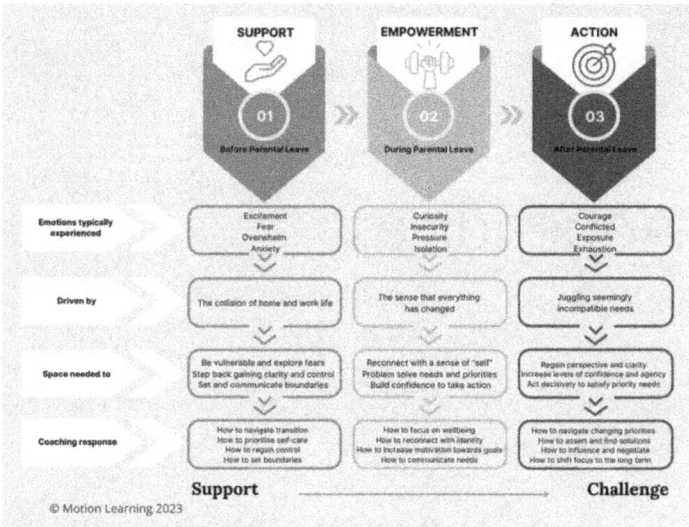

© Motion Learning 2023

Appendix B: Possible human values

Accomplishment	Calmness	Contentment
Achievement	Carefulness	Contribution
Adventure	Certainty	Cooperation
Affection	Challenge	Courage
Altruism	Cheerfulness	Creativity
Ambition	Commitment	Curiosity
Amusement	Common sense	Daring
Appreciation	Compassion	Decisiveness
Autonomy	Competence	Dependability
Awareness	Competition	Determination
Balance	Confidence	Dignity
Beauty	Conformity	Diligence
Belonging	Connection	Discipline
Benevolence	Conservation	Diversity
Bravery	Consistency	Duty

Ecstasy
Efficiency
Effort
Empathy
Endurance
Enjoyment
Enthusiasm
Excellence
Excitement
Experience
Expertise
Exploration
Fairness
Faith
Fame
Family
Fashion
Fidelity
Flexibility
Forgiveness
Freedom
Friendship
Fun
Generosity
Genuineness
Gratitude
Gregariousness
Happiness
Hard work
Harmony
Health
Honesty
Humility
Humour
Imagination
Impact

Impartiality
Independence
Individuality
Innovation
Integrity
Intelligence
Intuition
Inventiveness
Joy
Justice
Kindness
Knowledge
Learning
Liberty
Logic
Loyalty
Mastery
Mercy
Modesty
Nature
Non-conformity
Obedience
Open-mindedness
Optimism
Order
Originality
Passion
Patience
Peace
Perceptiveness
Perfection
Persistence
Personal growth
Perspective
Persuasiveness
Philanthropy

Playfulness
Popularity
Power
Pride
Privacy
Prudence
Purpose
Rationality
Realism
Reasoning
Recognition
Reflection
Relationships
Reliability
Reputation
Resilience
Respect
Responsibility
Security
Self-awareness
Self-control
Self-direction
Self-reliance
Self-respect
Sensuality
Serenity
Simplicity
Sincerity
Solitude
Spirituality
Spontaneity
Stability
Status
Thoroughness
Tradition
Tranquility

Transcendence	Variety	Wealth
Trust	Vision	Winning
Truth	Volunteering	Wisdom
Understanding	Warmth	

Motion Learning, 2023

Bibliography

Berne, E. *Games people play: The psychology of human relationships* (1968)

Bridges, W. *Managing transitions: Making the most of change* (2003)

Cialdini, R.B. *Influence: The psychology of persuasion* (2007)

Covey, S. *The 7 habits of highly effective people* (1989)

Csikszentmihalyi, M. *Flow: The psychology of happiness* (2013)

Goffee, R. and Jones, C. 'Why should anyone be led by you?', *Harvard Business Review*, September–October (2000)

Gordon, T. and Burch, N. *TET* (1974)

Govindji, Reena and Linley, P. 'Strengths use, self-concordance and well-being: Implications for strengths coaching and coaching psychologists'. *International Coaching Psychology Review* (2007)

Watkins, M. *The first 90 days: Critical success strategies for new leaders at all levels* (2003)

Further reading

Transition

Bridges, W. *Managing transitions: Making the most of change* (2009)

Samuel, J. *This too shall pass: Stories of change, crisis and hopeful beginnings* (2020)

Fear

Beaver, C. 'The chimp paradox'. *Literary Cultures*, 4(1) (2021)

Van der Kolk, B. *The body keeps the score: Mind, brain and body in the transformation of trauma* (2014)

Learning

Brown, B. *Brené Brown: The power of vulnerability*. TED Talk at www. ted.com/talks/brene_brown_the_power_of_vulnerability? language=en (2010)

Dweck, C. *Mindset-updated edition: Changing the way you think to fulfil your potential* (2017)

Control

Covey, S. *The 7 habits of highly effective people* (1989)

Rotter, J.B. 'Internal versus external control of reinforcement: A case history of a variable'. *American Psychologist*, 45(4) (1990)

Self-care

Seligman, M.E. *Flourish: A visionary new understanding of happiness and well-being* (2011)

Online self-care resources

Action for Happiness www.actionforhappiness.org

Mental Health Foundation www.mentalhealth.org.uk

NHS www.nhs.uk/mental-health/self-help/

University of Pennsylvania, Authentic Happiness Portal www.authentichappiness.sas.upenn.edu

Values – happiness – positive psychology

Boniwell, I. *Positive psychology in a nutshell: The science of happiness:* (2012)

Layard, R. *Happiness: Lessons from a new science* (2nd edn) (2011)

Seligman, M.E. *Authentic happiness: Using the new positive psychology to realize your potential for lasting fulfilment* (2002)

Strengths

Buckingham, M. and Clifton, D.O. *Now, discover your strengths* (2001)

Buckingham, M. *Go put your strengths to work: 6 powerful steps to achieve outstanding performance* (2007)

Goffee, R. and Jones, G. *Why should anyone be led by you?* (with new preface by the authors) (2015)

Motivation

Pink, D.H. *Drive: The surprising truth about what motivates us* (2011)

Sinek, S. *Start with why: The inspiring million-copy bestseller that will help you find your purpose* (2011)

Effectiveness

Csikszentmihalyi, M. *Flow: The psychology of happiness* (2013)

Csikszentmihalyi, M. *Flow: The psychology of optimal experience* (2008)

Kline, N. *Time to think: Listening to ignite the human mind* (1999)

Manson, M. *The subtle art of not giving a f*ck: A counterintuitive approach to living a good life* (2016)

Watkins, M. *The first 90 days: Critical success strategies for new leaders at all levels* (2003)

Communication

Berne, E. *Games people play: The psychology of human relationships* (1968)

Cialdini, R.B. *Influence: The psychology of persuasion* (2007)

Rosenberg, M.B. *Nonviolent communication: A language of compassion* (2002)

Coaching

Downey, M. *Effective coaching* (1999)

Peltier, B. *The psychology of executive coaching: Theory and application* (2001)

Rogers, J. *Coaching skills: The definitive guide to being a coach* (4th edn) (2016)

Schmidt, E., Rosenberg, J. and Eagle, A. *Trillion dollar coach: The leadership handbook of Silicon Valley's Bill Campbell* (2019)

Starr, J. *The coaching manual: The definitive guide to the process, principles, and skills of personal coaching* (2008)

Stober, D.R. and Grant, A. *Evidence-based coaching handbook: Putting best practices to work for your clients* (2006)

Whitmore, J. *Coaching for performance: GROWing human potential and purpose: The principles and practice of coaching and leadership* (2009)

About the author

Rachel Morris is a proud working mother.

Self-employed for more than 20 years as a professional business coach, Rachel returned to work when her first son was six weeks old. In doing this, she realized that not only did she need to, but that she wanted to. She loved being a mum deeply. She loved her work too.

Over the last ten years, Rachel has focused on understanding the parental transition experienced by working parents, identifying patterns and trends in behaviours.

Rachel wants to be part of creating a world for her children where parents are empowered to be great at work and at home. Should they choose to be.

Rachel is a leading thinker, writer and speaker in this space, and on a mission to share the critical insight she has gained. She can be contacted via www.workingmotherbook.com

Rachel is a founding partner of two coaching companies: Motion Learning, a professional business coaching company (www.motionlearning.com); and the not-for-profit 'Coach Community' (www.coachcommunity.org).

She lives in London, UK with her partner and two boys.

Index